MW00826226

—— ENSURING ——

High-Quality
Curriculum

ENSURING

High-Quality Curriculum

HOW TO

DESIGN

REVISE

OR

ADOPT

CURRICULUM ALIGNED TO
STUDENT SUCCESS

Alexandria, Virginia USA

1703 N. Beauregard St. • Alexandria, VA 22311-1714 USA
Phone: 800-933-2723 or 703-578-9600 • Fax: 703-575-5400
Website: www.ascd.org • E-mail: member@ascd.org
Author guidelines: www.ascd.org/write

Deborah S. Delisle, *Executive Director;* Robert D. Clouse, *Managing Director, Digital Content & Publications;* Stefani Roth, *Publisher;* Genny Ostertag, *Director, Content Acquisitions;* Julie Houtz, *Director, Book Editing & Production;* Miriam Calderone, *Editor;* Thomas Lytle, *Senior Graphic Designer;* Mike Kalyan, *Manager, Production Services;* Cynthia Stock, *Production Designer;* Andrea Wilson, *Senior Production Specialist*

Copyright © 2017 ASCD. All rights reserved. It is illegal to reproduce copies of this work in print or electronic format (including reproductions displayed on a secure intranet or stored in a retrieval system or other electronic storage device from which copies can be made or displayed) without the prior written permission of the publisher. By purchasing only authorized electronic or print editions and not participating in or encouraging piracy of copyrighted materials, you support the rights of authors and publishers. Readers who wish to reproduce or republish excerpts of this work in print or electronic format may do so for a small fee by contacting the Copyright Clearance Center (CCC), 222 Rosewood Dr., Danvers, MA 01923, USA (phone: 978-750-8400; fax: 978-646-8600; web: www.copyright.com). To inquire about site licensing options or any other reuse, contact ASCD Permissions at www.ascd.org/permissions, or permissions@ascd.org, or 703-575-5749. For a list of vendors authorized to license ASCD e-books to institutions, see www.ascd.org/epubs. Send translation inquiries to translations@ascd.org.

ASCD® and ASCD LEARN. TEACH. LEAD.® are registered trademarks of ASCD. All other trademarks contained in this book are the property of, and reserved by, their respective owners, and are used for editorial and informational purposes only. No such use should be construed to imply sponsorship or endorsement of the book by the respective owners.

Excerpts from Common Core State Standards © Copyright 2010. National Governors Association Center for Best Practices and Council of Chief State School Officers. All rights reserved.

All web links in this book are correct as of the publication date below but may have become inactive or otherwise modified since that time. If you notice a deactivated or changed link, please e-mail books@ascd.org with the words "Link Update" in the subject line. In your message, please specify the web link, the book title, and the page number on which the link appears.

PAPERBACK ISBN: 978-1-4166-2279-6   ASCD product #116006   n10/16
PDF E-BOOK ISBN: 978-1-4166-2281-9; see Books in Print for other formats.

Quantity discounts: 10–49, 10%; 50+, 15%; 1,000+, special discounts (e-mail programteam@ascd.org or call 800-933-2723, ext. 5773, or 703-575-5773). For desk copies, go to www.ascd.org/deskcopy.

Library of Congress Cataloging-in-Publication Data
Names: Lalor, Angela Di Michele, author.
Title: Ensuring high-quality curriculum : how to design, revise, or adopt
   curriculum aligned to student success / Angela Di Michele Lalor.
Description: Alexandria, VA : ASCD, [2017] | Includes bibliographical
   references and index.
Identifiers: LCCN 2016033240 (print) | LCCN 2016039839 (ebook) | ISBN
   9781416622796 (pbk.) | ISBN 9781416622819
   (PDF)
Subjects: LCSH: Curriculum planning.
Classification: LCC LB2806.15 .L35 2017 (print) | LCC LB2806.15 (ebook) | DDC
   375/.001—dc23
LC record available at https://lccn.loc.gov/2016033240

23 22 21 20 19   3 4 5 6 7 8 9 10 11 12

To my children, William, Catherine, and Joseph,
so that they learn anything is possible, and to my
mother, Jessie Di Michele, who taught me that it is.

—— ENSURING ——

High-Quality
Curriculum

HOW TO DESIGN, REVISE, OR ADOPT CURRICULUM
ALIGNED TO STUDENT SUCCESS

Acknowledgments viii

Introduction: The "Big Picture" of Curriculum 1

Consideration 1: Organizing Centers 9

Consideration 2: Alignment to Standards 24

Consideration 3: Standards Placement and Emphasis 46

Consideration 4: Assessment Types and Purposes 66

Consideration 5: Curriculum-Embedded Performance
    Assessments 84

Consideration 6: Instruction 111

Consideration 7: Resources That Support Instruction 136

Consideration 8: Success with Your Curriculum 155

Epilogue 173

Appendix A 176

Appendix B 184

References 202

Index 205

About the Author 210

Related ASCD Resources 212

Acknowledgments

This book would not be complete without acknowledging the many people who have inspired and supported me.

The consultants at Learner-Centered Initiatives have been unwavering in their support, not only in being part of the process but also in their belief that I had something worthy to say. I have learned so much from Giselle Martin-Kniep, Joanne Picone-Zocchia, Diane Cunningham, and Jennifer Borgioli.

It is from the school administrators, teachers, and coaches with whom I have worked during the last 20 years that I have learned about good, quality teaching and what it means to make a difference in the lives of students. I thank those who let me include their work in this book and all those whom I have worked with and learned from along the way.

I would like to acknowledge my personal cheerleader and lifelong friend Kathleen Wallace. I would also like to share my appreciation for the continuing support of my parents, Mike and Jessie Di Michele, and I would especially like to thank my husband, Bill, and my children, William, Catherine, and Joseph, who may not have always known what I was doing on the computer but gave me the space to do it.

The "Big Picture" of Curriculum

"The 2nd grade teachers have common planning time once a month where they map out what they will be teaching."

"The curriculum writing team will be meeting on Thursdays after school."

"Please submit a list of recommendations for read-aloud books that support the social studies curriculum."

"The school board has approved the adoption of a new reading program."

These quotes capture the many and diverse ways that schools approach curriculum. Designing, adopting, or revising curriculum can be viewed as an exciting opportunity or a daunting task. An educator's perspective is based on each individual's prior experiences working with curriculum as well as that person's personal view as to what constitutes quality. When individuals are then put into groups to adopt or design a curriculum, as is often the case, it becomes very difficult for them to do so. Often the result is an unwieldy and unmanageable curriculum, the purchase of a program that does not quite match up with what a district needs or values, or some variation in between.

My experiences facilitating professional development programs related to curriculum led me to see a need for a book devoted to curriculum that readers would be able to use to guide the curriculum design process and evaluate curriculum in a meaningful and manageable way. Most books about curriculum are devoted to the design and examination of individual units of study that sit within the curriculum. What makes this book different is that it examines the "big picture" of curriculum—what needs to be considered when all the units are put together. By examining the big picture, educators can determine the curriculum's strengths and weaknesses, and they can decide where to focus attention in its design and revision or where to supplement when adopting a published curriculum. And there *will* be a need for evaluation and revision, because the statement "curriculum is a living document" is amply true. In fact, considering a curriculum "done" is really an indicator that it is time to revisit the curriculum again.

Layers of Curriculum

To begin the process of evaluating and designing curriculum, we first must define what we mean by curriculum. Traditionally, curriculum is thought of as the *what* in teaching—what students learn in school. It sounds simple enough, but what students learn is multilayered and can be interpreted as many things, including content, skills and strategies, processes, books and resources, and dispositions and habits of mind. To clarify the *what*, it is helpful to look at the different layers of curriculum (Martin-Kniep, 1999):

- *Formal curriculum* describes what students need to know, be able to do, and value.
- *Operational curriculum* translates formal curriculum into a plan for instruction.
- *Taught curriculum* is what is delivered in the classroom.
- *Assessed curriculum* is what is evaluated through formal measures.
- *Learned curriculum* is what students walk away understanding as a result of their learning experiences.

Formal Curriculum

When we hear the word *curriculum*, typically what we picture is the formal curriculum. Formal curriculum describes what students need to know, be able to do, and be like through statements in the form of national and local standards, content-specific understandings and practices, district- or teacher-generated outcomes and objectives, and other types of learning targets. Standards have different focuses but generally fall into three categories: process, content, and disposition. Process standards focus on skills and strategies, content standards identify either content-specific skills and practices or subject-specific information, and dispositional standards address ways of thinking or habits of mind.

Although standards have been used to guide classroom practice for many years, the Common Core State Standards (CCSS) have brought renewed attention to the standards-based design process and cause to revisit curriculum. The CCSS in English language arts (ELA) and literacy are an example of process standards. They lay out what students should be able to do at each grade level and are scaffolded from one grade level to the next, with each grade level building on the skills and processes from the previous grade level. They do not, however, prescribe the content that needs to be taught.

Content information can be gathered from other formal curriculum documents. For example, in New York State, social studies teachers use the CCLS (New York State's version of the CCSS) to guide reading and writing processes but use the state Social Studies Framework (New York State K–12 Social Studies Framework, n.d.) for guidelines regarding social studies content and practices specific to the discipline. The Next Generation Science Standards (NGSS, 2013) are content standards that articulate content, science and engineering practices, and crosscutting concepts.

Cognitive processes, social and work habits, and thinking demands or dispositions can also serve as formal curriculum because they describe what students should be like or express what is valued in learning. Often these cognitive processes or ways of thinking are not articulated through standards but rather through formal descriptions, scales, or progressions such as Bloom's taxonomy, habits of mind (Costa & Kallick, 2000), and executive function skills. In this book, categorical descriptions such as these are referenced as standards.

Regardless of focus, formal curriculum describes what the learner needs to know, be able to do, and value. The key word here is *learner*. It is the responsibility of the school and teachers to ensure that students have the opportunity to learn and demonstrate the content, skills, processes, and dispositions embedded within the standards, and this responsibility, in turn, generates the need for an operational curriculum.

Operational Curriculum

Standards lay out priorities and serve as the driving force behind the curriculum, answering the question *Why do we have to teach that?* However, by themselves standards cannot be used in the classroom; they must be made operational. The operational curriculum brings together different types of standards, content, texts, and resources. It identifies ways to assess student learning and provides appropriate learning experiences that can be used during instruction.

There has been a great deal of confusion about the formal curriculum and the operational curriculum. Formal curriculum does not dictate specifics such as the texts students will read or the type of animal to be studied when learning about habitats. Those specifics are identified in the operational curriculum, and in a quality curriculum, they should reflect the values and priorities of the community the curriculum serves. Standards are designed to ensure that all students have the same skills and use the same processes, whereas curriculum identifies what content and resources they will be using to do so.

Taught, Assessed, and Learned Curriculum

Through the operational curriculum, teachers make decisions about what occurs in the classroom and implement the taught curriculum. Many factors affect this decision-making process, including time, interest, and makeup of the student body. Given that no teacher and group of students are ever the same from one classroom to the next, the taught curriculum will not be exactly the same in every classroom. It is unreasonable to assume that all teachers of the same grade level will be teaching exactly the same thing, the same way, on the same day. A quality curriculum will provide the information that teachers require to make purposeful decisions to meet student needs and provide the appropriate pathway for meeting the expectations outlined in the operational curriculum without dictating a one-way-suits-all approach.

Through the assessed curriculum, teachers are able to determine what the students have and have not learned, identify areas of strengths and needs, and make decisions about next steps in instruction. Once again, choices are made as to what is assessed. A quality curriculum includes assessments that closely align to the standards and big ideas found in each unit. A quality curriculum will also include different types of assessments so teachers can accurately determine the learned curriculum—what students know and understand as a result of instruction—and how well student understanding aligns with the formal curriculum.

With so many layers in the curriculum, it is easy to see how standards can get "lost in translation." Students do not always leave the classroom understanding the skills, processes, and content that have been identified in the formal curriculum. Although many factors affect learning, one that we do have control over is the use of the formal curriculum to create a purposefully aligned, engaging, and meaningful curriculum for our students.

How This Book Is Organized

This book is organized in five sections similar to the steps in a standards-based design process used to create curriculum: organizational structure, standards, assessment, instruction, and format. The chapters in each section focus on a specific consideration for the creation and examination of curriculum. They provide a detailed look at what you need to consider when you are examining or designing quality curriculum, and they include many examples and illustrations from different schools, content areas, and grade levels. (In addition, Appendix B walks you through an annotated 6th grade math unit to demonstrate how the attributes of quality curriculum apply to mathematics.) Within each chapter are tools and activities to help you further understand the attributes of a quality curriculum and, more important, to help you evaluate or plan your own curriculum and give you feedback as to what areas warrant further investigation. Each chapter ends with a summary, a brief recap of the tools and activities presented in the chapter, and a checklist that you can use during the evaluation or design process.

Organizational Structure of Curriculum

Consideration 1—Organizing Centers. The first area to consider when designing or evaluating curriculum is the organizing center. A unit's organizing center is communicated through its title, essential question, and big idea. A quality curriculum will organize units of study around centers that are worthy of the time and energy set aside for their pursuit and that reflect the overall intent and purpose of the curriculum. This chapter examines the various components that make up the organizing center for a unit and provides a simple tool and guiding questions that will help you to examine or plan the organizing centers for your curriculum.

Standards

Consideration 2—Alignment to Standards. As many teachers reconsider their curriculum because of the adoption of new standards, it is worthwhile to first examine the curriculum to determine how well the assessments and learning experiences align to the standards. Too often a curriculum lists standards in a way that denotes equal importance, and the curriculum user or writer accepts that tasks align to the standards in equal measure. This chapter focuses on the importance of examining how standards are communicated within a curriculum and provides activities that will help you determine the degree of alignment between tasks and standards.

Consideration 3—Standards Placement and Emphasis. Another consideration when examining standards is how they are placed within the

curriculum; order does matter. When determining placement and emphasis, it is important to consider factors such as the overall intent of the
standards, grade-level focus standards, gradual release of responsibility,
and developmentally appropriate practice. This chapter explores each of
the factors in detail and provides you with a choice of standards-analysis
tools that are helpful in evaluating the placement of standards within the
curriculum or when planning for design.

Assessment

Consideration 4—Assessment Types and Purposes. Teachers use four
types of assessments to determine what students know, are able to do, and
value. The types are information recall, demonstration, product assessment, and process assessment. A quality curriculum includes different
types of assessments that are congruent with the standards for the unit.
Teachers use these various assessments at different moments to ascertain
what students know and are able to do. A quality curriculum will therefore
include diagnostic assessments as well as assessments used for formative
and summative purposes. This chapter explores the role of different types
of assessments and the purposes they serve within a curriculum.

Consideration 5—Curriculum-Embedded Performance Assessments. A
quality curriculum will include assessments that produce as well as measure learning. This chapter presents criteria for high-quality curriculum-
embedded performance assessments that serve this purpose. These
assessments measure the most important learning for the unit, are congruent with and strongly align to standards, have an authentic audience
and purpose, and include diagnostic and formative assessment moments.

Instruction

Consideration 6—Instruction. Learning experiences and lessons are two
ways to communicate what should be taught daily. Either structure should
include information about what students will do, why they will do it, and
what the teacher will have as evidence of student learning. These lessons
and learning experiences should be strongly aligned to the standards for

that unit. A quality curriculum includes learning experiences or lessons that address content, process, and dispositions. This chapter provides strategies for ensuring the use of different types of lessons and learning experiences and includes information to guide instruction.

Consideration 7—Resources That Support Instruction. Resources include texts, technology, and materials that support instruction. The guiding principle behind the selection of these materials is how they will serve the purpose of the learning experience. This chapter offers guiding questions to assist you in the selection of resources to support the curriculum.

Format

Consideration 8—Success with Your Curriculum. This chapter reiterates the information provided throughout the book and offers three final thoughts for successfully implementing and using your curriculum. A quality curriculum is easily accessible to teachers and other educators who use it, is supported by professional development, and is connected to student work. Included in this chapter are examples, guiding questions, and student work protocols to help you successfully implement your curriculum.

Organizing Centers

Which unit within each of the following example sets captures your attention?

Example Set 1

A. *The Grapes of Wrath* and the Great Depression: Students read *The Grapes of Wrath* by John Steinbeck and write a report on the Great Depression.

B. Literature or Life? In this unit students study the essential question *What's more real—literature or life?*They read several poems, short stories, and a full-length novel to analyze the connection between the time period in which the works were written and the events of the time. Students use their understanding of this connection to write their own review and analysis of a contemporary novel and how it reflects the lifestyle and values of today.

Example Set 2

A. Goods and Services: Students learn the difference between businesses in their community that sell goods and those that provide services. Based on what they have learned, they sort pictures of different businesses into the two categories.

B. The Business of Business: *What do you do?* Students understand that businesses provide different types of goods and services. They explore different types of businesses by analyzing those in their own local community and conducting additional research on the goods and services provided by businesses online. Students prepare and conduct an interview with a local businessperson about the goods or services that individual provides for the community. Students use their understanding of goods and services and information they learned from their interview to write a proposal suggesting an idea for a new store or website that would provide a good or a service that their age group or family would find appealing.

Example Set 3

A. Habit of Mind 12—Wonderment and Awe: In this unit students study the habit of mind "wonderment and awe" (Costa & Kallick, 2000). They learn what this habit of mind means and find examples of how it exists in the world around them and in themselves.

B. Wonderment and Awe: *How do you see the world?* In this unit, students explore the habit of mind "wonderment and awe" and how it affects the way people see the world. They find examples and nonexamples of how wonderment and awe affect a person's views of text, art, music, and the natural world. Students end the unit by selecting a visual art form and using it to show how they see the world with wonderment and awe.

Sometimes first impressions do matter, and the way in which a curriculum first communicates what it values is through its organizing center. An organizing center is the central idea upon which a unit of study is built. It can be a topic, a theme, a concept, an issue, a problem, a process, or a phenomenon (Martin-Kniep, 2000). An organizing center is communicated through a unit's title, essential question, and big idea. A quality curriculum will organize units of study around centers that are worthy of the time and energy set aside for their pursuit and that reflect the overall intent and purpose of the curriculum.

So the question becomes, What is the best way to organize the curriculum? If you review the examples just provided, you can see the impact that decision has on the curriculum.

In the first example set, the same unit is organized around a text and a related topic, and then a simple question. The first organizational structure, Unit A of the set, limits the scope of the unit to a particular text (*The Grapes of Wrath*) and topic (the Great Depression). More than likely, students will be led through an in-depth analysis of the text with references to their research on the Dust Bowl and the Great Depression. The unit has not been intentionally designed to make the leap from *The Grapes of Wrath* to other texts and time periods and to the larger question posed in Unit B: *What's more real—literature or life?*

In Unit B, students have the opportunity to examine the connection between literature and life, contemplating the role of fictional accounts in understanding real events and time periods. Although *The Grapes of Wrath* can still be a central text, teachers will likely want to consider additional works from other time periods, including *To Kill a Mockingbird,* by Harper Lee; *The Great Gatsby,* by F. Scott Fitzgerald; and *The Catcher in the Rye,* by J. D. Salinger. Each text allows students to examine how literature reflects real life and prepares them for an analysis of a contemporary work.

The units described in the second example set are from a financial literacy curriculum for elementary students. Unit A approaches the curriculum in a direct manner. The organizing center is the topic students will be studying: goods and services. In Unit A, students learn to distinguish between businesses that sell goods and those that provide services. Unit B identifies the context for the examination of goods and services by identifying the bigger idea of businesses. It personalizes the unit through the essential question *What do you do?*—a common question posed by adults among their peers. Although both units may have students engaging in similar activities, such as examining the types of goods and services provided in the community, only Unit B requires that students apply their understanding in a new and novel way.

In the third example set, the units come from a curriculum developed around the habits of mind articulated by Costa and Kallick (2000). Unit A is structured to present "wonderment and awe" as one in a series. Unit

B links the habit to an essential question, showing how wonderment and awe can affect the student and moving the unit from abstract to practical. The essential question lends itself to exploration across media and content, bringing in literature, art, music, and science.

In each example set, Unit B

- Moves away from a topic to a bigger idea, concept, or essential question.
- Can be explored from different perspectives, across content, place, or time.
- Is relevant and meaningful because it results in the application to something bigger than school.
- Requires higher levels of thinking by asking students to analyze, evaluate, and create.

Organizing Centers in the Content Areas

The same principle of organizing centers applies to content areas. Let's look at a social studies unit to see the impact of three different organizing centers on the same unit of study. Typically social studies units are organized around topics such as the American Revolution. Students know that in such a unit they will learn about the war. Instruction will focus on the events that led to the war, the major battles, and the ultimate results. The unit stays within the context of that event, in that time, in that place.

Let's see what happens when the organizing center moves from topic to concept and the unit explores rebellions and revolutions. Now the unit lends itself to the exploration of other events. With this organizing center, the students first take a look at the American Revolution and then examine other events in American history that fall under the heading Rebellions and Revolutions. These events could include the Whiskey Rebellion, Shays Rebellion, the War of 1812, Nat Turner's rebellion, and John Brown's raid, to name a few.

content center: topic / concept / essential question

A third approach to teaching these topics is to examine the same events through an organizing center of an essential question: *Rebellion or revolution?* This example differs slightly from the other two. Rather than focusing solely on the events, this essential question requires students to evaluate the events taught in the unit of study through different points of view. For example, in their examination of the American Revolution, students might examine how the British and the Loyalists viewed the events leading to the war and the war itself as acts of rebellion against the British king and parliament. At the same time, the Sons of Liberty, the patriots, and eventually the Continental Congress felt they had legitimate cause to sever ties with Great Britain and form their own country, hence the naming of the American Revolution. Similar studies of point of view and cause and effect are examined as they relate to each of the subsequent events, asking students to determine the legitimacy of the name given to the event and the way it is presented in history books—and, more important, establishing a set of criteria with which to examine rebellion and revolution in the world today.

Essential Questions

The unit title communicates the focus and importance of the unit, but it does not stand alone in identifying the organizing center. The organizing center is further explained by the unit's essential question.

Which of the following two groups of questions are essential? How do they differ from each other?

Group A
- What makes a story last?
- How do you measure success? .
- What is more constant than change?
- Is beauty in the eye of the beholder?
- Are all leaders great?

Group B — *guiding questions*

- How do folktales and fables share a lesson or moral?
- How do you describe the characters in the story?
- What is erosion?
- How do poems incorporate similes and metaphors?
- What were the contributions of the American presidents?

The questions in Group A would be considered *essential questions* because they are large, global questions that can be explored and contemplated, elicit multiple perspectives, and do not require one correct answer. In Jay McTighe and Grant Wiggins's book on essential questions, these questions would be considered "overarching" essential questions (McTighe & Wiggins, 2013).

In a quality unit of study, the essential question provides the context and direction for the unit. It poses the focus of exploration as it relates to the unit title and in some cases serves as the title itself. If the essential question changed, the unit would go in a different direction, as seen in the social studies example just presented.

The essential questions in Group A are different from the questions in Group B, which are *guiding questions*. Although still important for articulating what students will examine in a unit of study, guiding questions are answerable and do not communicate the organizing center of the unit. Guiding questions identify the important skills, content, and dispositions of the unit and are used to create the classroom learning activities.

The Central or Big Idea

The central or big idea is a statement that identifies the most important learning of the unit in a clear and concise manner. Often it articulates a generalization related to the essential question and serves as the connector between the essential question and the unit title, as seen in the following examples:

Example 1

Unit Title: Civilizations: Old and New

Essential Question: What makes a civilization classical?

Big Idea: Students understand that classical civilizations share common characteristics and have left unique contributions that still affect us today.

Example 2

Unit Title: Homes for Everyone and Everything

Essential Question: Why is a home important?

Big Idea: Students understand that home is an important concept to all living species and that environmental challenges can affect a living species' ability to survive and thrive in its home.

The big idea communicates the overall outcome for the unit. Without it, the curriculum user would need to examine all of the curriculum components to determine the desired results, often resulting in multiple users having different interpretations. With clear articulation of the big idea, all users understand the importance of the unit—a consequence that is particularly valuable when it comes time for assessment, because the performance task is designed to measure the most important learning for the unit.

Implications for Evaluating, Creating, or Revising Curriculum

Although it may seem like the organizing center plays a minor role in the overall curriculum design and evaluation process, examining or determining the organizing center is an important first step. Keeping in mind that this book is about the "big picture" of curriculum, it is important to look beyond the first unit of study or the unit of study you are currently working on and examine or identify *all* the organizing centers for the curriculum to determine if they convey the message you want to send about what you value in curriculum.

An example from my work in P.S. 11 in New York City illustrates how examining and revising the organizing center can affect the overall curriculum. The principal, Dr. Joan Kong, invited me to work with the school's coach, Angela Miuta, and a group of teachers—Hande Williams, Teresa Ranieri, Thalia Jackson-Cole, Elvira Gonzalez, and Laura Magnotta—to assist them in using the New York State Common Core Learning Standards to design their own curriculum. The group engaged in a recursive process of design and revision based on implementation, and after several years of doing so they had to choose a textbook for English language arts. Because **textbooks do not serve as curriculum,** the group sat down to evaluate the new series and determine what needed to be done to make it their own. The following examples from the 4th grade curriculum illustrate what they found.

> **Unit 1: Animal Structure**—*How does an animal's structure help it to live?* Students read informational texts about animals to compare, gather, and synthesize ideas. After doing so, they create an infographic on an animal by describing the animal's physical characteristics, its habitat, and special adaptations.

> **Unit 2: Regions of the United States**—*How are the regions of the United States unique?* Students read informational texts about the unique regions of the United States. Students write an opinion sharing reasons as to why one of the regions would be the best place to live.

> **Unit 3: Earth**—*How has the Earth's surface changed?* Students read informational texts to develop an understanding of how the Earth's surface has changed. After doing so, students write a comparative essay that examines the effects of change to the Earth's surface as explained in a paired myth passage.

> **Unit 4: America's Economy**—*How does the economy work?* Students read literary texts to determine how different characters have worked to overcome challenges in meeting their needs. Students use this information to write a narrative in which a character meets a need.

Examining the organizing centers for each unit sent clear messages about the overall organizing center for the curriculum:

- The curriculum was organized by topics related to content areas.
- The organizing center for each unit was communicated through a title and an answerable guiding question.
- The curriculum separated the study of fiction and nonfiction text by units.
- The culminating tasks for each unit were designed with the teacher as the sole audience for student work.

The school, however, was looking for a curriculum that integrated English language arts with content in a meaningful way, included units that allowed for the examination of fiction and nonfiction simultaneously, and provided the opportunity for students to engage in authentic and meaningful tasks. Given that the school did not have a choice in resources, the teachers set out to make the curriculum their own and planned a curriculum using what they had learned about the organizing centers. The result was the following:

Unit 1: Survival—*What does it take to survive?* Students understand that survival is a recurring theme in literature and in life. Students read survival stories to identify and explain traits of characters who have survived physical challenges and other obstacles. They read informational texts about how animals adapt and survive in their different habitats. Students choose an animal to research and create an infographic for younger students explaining the survival instincts of the animals.

Unit 2: Regions—*Does where you live matter?* Students read informational text about the different regions of the United States and fictional stories set in these different regions. After reading the stories, they determine the impact the setting had on the story. Students choose one of the regions and create a resource that could be used by individuals who are deciding whether they should move to that region.

Unit 3: Natural Phenomena— *What really happens?* Students understand that over time both traditional stories and science have been used to explain how natural phenomena occur. Students read myths, folktales, and fables to learn how these traditional stories have been used to explain natural phenomena in different times and places. They read nonfiction texts that explain the science behind these occurrences. As a result of this unit, students write an introduction to a myth, folktale, or fable found in the school library in which they explain the connection between the science and the story.

Unit 4: Innovative Solutions— *What does it take to be innovative?* Students understand that innovative ideas often lead to creative solutions to personal, economic, and other types of problems. In this unit, students read fiction and nonfiction texts, including stories, editorials, and news articles, that provide examples of how people have used innovative solutions to solve problems. Together the class creates a definition of what it means to be innovative. The students identify problems that they have encountered in their own lives and choose one as the basis for writing a proposal that identifies an innovative solution that they can carry out as a class to solve the problem.

The result of the school's work was a curriculum that reflected the criteria the teachers had established and that communicated what they valued. The lesson to be learned from this school is that there are steps you can take in the early stages of choosing or evaluating a curriculum, as well as when planning to design your own, that result in a curriculum that reflects what you value for your students.

Figure 1.1 is a tool that you can use for evaluation and planning. The chart contains space for six units of study and can be modified to reflect the number of units in the curriculum you are evaluating. Typically a year's curriculum can include six units, each approximately six weeks long. However, the length of a unit should be based on what students will learn and do, so all units may not require the same amount of time.

Figure 1.1
EVALUATING ORGANIZING CENTERS

Titles (List unit titles here.)	Unit Description (Identify any essential questions and big ideas; describe what students will learn or do during the unit.)
Unit 1:	
Unit 2:	
Unit 3:	
Unit 4:	
Unit 5:	
Unit 6:	

Once you have identified the information called for in Figure 1.1, you can use it to answer the following questions and evaluate the organizing centers for the curriculum:

• What are the recurring organizing centers used for each unit of study—topic, theme, concept, issue, problem, process, or phenomenon?

• How are the organizing centers articulated within the curriculum—title only; title and essential question; or title, essential question, and big idea?

• How do the organizing centers align to the values and focuses of the school as articulated through one or more of the following: the school's mission and vision statement, the process and content standards, the learning processes, and the dispositions and habits of mind that are used to guide instruction?

• How do the organizing centers support student learning by creating appeal and then engaging students in meaningful, purposeful, and authentic experiences?

If the organizing center is narrow in focus, is articulated only through the title, and does not allow for in-depth analysis or reflect the values and focuses of the school, it is an early indicator that this may not be the curriculum for you or that your existing curriculum needs revising. If you are designing your own curriculum, it is important to consider these questions before you begin.

Choosing the "Right" Organizing Centers

There is no one "right" organizing center for all schools. Answering the questions just listed will help you identify the right organizing centers for *your* curriculum. The most important of those questions is *How do the organizing centers align to the values and focuses of the school?* School values and focuses are communicated in many ways, including through the

- School's mission and vision statement.
- Process and content standards that have been adopted by the state or local school board.
- Learning processes that have been the focus of school, grade-level, or department collegial circles and professional development.
- Dispositions and habits of mind used by the school to guide student metacognition.

Figure 1.2 includes several examples to illustrate the connection between school values and focuses and the organizing center for the curriculum.

Summary: Organizing Centers

An organizing center is the central idea upon which a unit of study is built. It is communicated through a unit's title, essential question, and big idea. Quality organizing centers are built around themes, concepts, issues, problems, processes, or phenomena. They align to the values of the school as articulated through one or more of the following: the school's mission and vision statement, the process and content standards, the learning processes, and the dispositions and habits of mind that are used to guide instruction. A quality curriculum will organize units of study around

Figure 1.2
CONNECTING SCHOOL VALUES AND FOCUSES WITH ORGANIZING CENTERS

School Values and Focuses as Articulated Through . . .	Related Organizing Center	Explanation
Example 1: Mission State-ment—We believe that students should learn in a safe, sup-portive, and student-centered environment. We are commit-ted to meeting the needs of all students, helping them to achieve academic excellence, and preparing them for a global society.	Schooling for All: *Does everyone deserve an edu-cation?* Students understand that not all children receive an education and how the lack of education affects the lives of those who don't.	This school's mission statement articulates the following goals for its students: • Safe, student-centered learn-ing environment that meets the need of all learners • Academic excellence • Preparation for a global society The related organizing center connects to the school's mission statement because it provides students with the opportunity to learn about education in other communities.
Example 2: Social Studies Themes—The National Council for the Social Studies identifies the following themes: • Culture • Time, Continuity, and Change • People, Places, and the Environment • Individual Development and Identity • Individuals, Groups, and Institutions • Power, Authority, and Governance • Production, Distribution, and Consumption • Science, Technology, and Society • Global Connections • Civic Ideals and Practices	Science, Technol-ogy, and Society: *Should science be controlled?* Stu-dents learn about the complexity of government regu-lation of scientific research because of religious, ethical, and moral issues.	The conceptually based social studies themes can easily be used as titles and narrowed in focus to specific grade-level content through the essential question and big idea. The concept of Science, Technology, and Society can be used as the unit title but is made more specific through the essential question and big idea.

(continues)

Figure 1.2

CONNECTING SCHOOL VALUES AND FOCUSES WITH ORGANIZING CENTERS (continued)

School Values and Focuses as Articulated Through . . .	Related Organizing Center	Explanation
Example 3: Common Core State Standards: • RI.11-12.4 Determine the meaning of words and phrases as they are used in a text, including figurative, connotative, and technical meanings; analyze how an author uses and refines the meaning of a key term or terms over the course of a text (e.g., how Madison defines *faction* in Federalist No. 10). • RI.11-12.5 Analyze and evaluate the effectiveness of the structure an author uses in his or her exposition or argument, including whether the structure makes points clear, convincing, and engaging. • RI.11-12.6 Determine an author's point of view or purpose in a text in which the rhetoric is particularly effective, analyzing how style and content contribute to the power, persuasiveness, or beauty of the text.	The Power of Words: *Can we make a difference with what we say?* Students explore how authors have used language and structure to communicate strong messages that have changed how people think about the world around them.	Analysis of the Common Core State Standards for reading informational text in 11th and 12th grade in comparison with those in 9th and 10th grade indicates that the following skills should be emphasized: • Analyze how an author uses and refines the meaning of a key term or terms over the course of a text. • Analyze and evaluate the effectiveness of the structure an author uses in her exposition or argument, including whether the structure makes points that are clear, convincing, and engaging. • Analyze how style and content contribute to the power, persuasiveness, or beauty of the text. The organizing center for the sample unit focuses on these skills by emphasizing the impact of language and structure on a text.

centers that are worthy of the time and energy set aside for their pursuit and that reflect the overall intent and purpose of the curriculum.

Tools and Activities for Evaluation, Design, and Revision

- **Evaluating Organizing Centers.** This tool (Figure 1.1) can be used either to identify organizing centers for a curriculum that is currently being designed or to evaluate the organizing centers in an existing curriculum. Using it to plan or evaluate the curriculum will ensure that the curriculum is on the right track and reflects the values of the school.

✔ Checklist for Evaluation, Design, and Revision

- ☐ The organizing center is articulated through the title, essential question, and big idea.

- ☐ The organizing center for each unit of study is a theme, a concept, an issue, a problem, a process, or a phenomenon.

- ☐ The organizing center aligns to the values of the school as articulated through one or more of the following: the school's mission and vision statement, the process and content standards, the learning processes, and the dispositions and habits of mind that are used to guide instruction.

- ☐ The organizing center supports student learning by creating appeal and will result in students engaging in meaningful, purposeful, and authentic experiences.

Alignment to Standards

Students sit in small groups reading different versions of the story *Stone Soup*. At one table students are examining the 1947 version of *Stone Soup* by Marcia Brown. In this story, three hungry soldiers enter a village looking for something to eat. The villagers hide their food until the soldiers slowly convince them to share it as they create a soup from stones. At another table, students are examining the later version by Jon J. Muth, which tells the story of three monks in China who face a similar situation when passing through a small village. Simultaneously, students at the remaining tables work with other versions of the same tale. Regardless of the version, all the students are identifying and discussing key details of the text as those details unfold, and the lesson they learned as a result, in preparation for a class discussion on the central message of the story.

Why are the students doing this? Their teacher has designed a learning experience to align to the Common Core standard for 3rd grade: *RL.3.2 Recount stories, including fables, folktales, and myths from diverse cultures; determine the central message, lesson, or moral and explain how it is conveyed through key details in the text.* Is the task, however, truly aligned to the standard?

After determining whether the curriculum is structured using organizing centers that reflect school values or focuses (the topic of Chapter 1), the next step in evaluating or creating a curriculum is to <u>ensure that it</u>

is strongly aligned to the standards the district uses to communicate its values and focuses and to guide instruction. In the classroom described here, if the students were simply asked to identify the main characters in the story, we could easily say that the task was not aligned to the standard. In most cases, examples and nonexamples of alignment are readily distinguishable from each other, making it easy to spot a curriculum that is not aligned. However, the evaluation of alignment is often not about whether a task is aligned or not but rather *to what degree.* In this case the question is, to what degree did the students' examination of the text align to the standard related to recounting key details from stories to determine the central message of the story? The answer is that the learning experience is strongly aligned to the standard. Students are completing work using the skills embedded in the standard. The focus of this chapter is to explore alignment and how to evaluate or create a curriculum that is strongly aligned to standards.

Degrees of Alignment

When examining a task that sits inside a learning experience or an assessment for degree of alignment, I suggest using a scale of weak, moderate, and strong. Weak alignment is evident when a task addresses only part of a standard or the underlying skills subsumed by the standard. For example, consider the following Common Core standard for 7th grade:

RL.7.5   Analyze how a drama's or poem's form or structure
           (e.g., soliloquy, sonnet) contributes to its meaning.

An example of a weakly aligned task would be one in which the students are asked to identify the pattern for the sonnet "How do I love thee? Let me count the ways" by Elizabeth Barrett Browning. One could argue that knowing that a sonnet is a 14-line poem divided into two sections—an 8-line stanza (octave) rhyming ABBAABBA, and a 6-line stanza (sestet) rhyming CDCDCD or CDEEDE—is helpful in identifying one. However, the task certainly does not get to the heart of the standard, which is to analyze how structure contributes to meaning. It may serve as a stepping stone to arriving at the standard, but as a task by itself it does not accomplish its goal.

Consider a task in which students are asked to write the message of the sonnet in one sentence. In this case, the task moves closer to the standard because students are analyzing the poem for its meaning. The teacher who designed the task considered structure, in that a sonnet focuses on one thought or idea, hence the request that students write a sentence. However, the task only moderately aligns to the standard because the students are not asked to make the connection between the structure of a sonnet and its meaning. The teacher has done that for them. The task may be used as a learning experience to reinforce the idea that a sonnet focuses on one idea, but again, left as an isolated task it cannot be considered strongly aligned to the standard.

In a strongly aligned task, students are asked to examine several sonnets for their structure and uncover what distinguishes a sonnet from other types of poems. Their examination of the sonnets leads to the understanding that a sonnet is a 14-line poem that focuses on a single thought or sentiment, and sonnets vary in that some are structured in two stanzas versus one and they may have different rhyming patterns. Students use their criteria to then analyze "How do I love thee? Let me count the ways." They work in groups to discuss how the structure affects the poem's message. Students consolidate their thinking in a written response that analyzes the impact of the structure on the meaning of the poem. In this example, the task is strongly aligned; it is difficult to separate the task from the standard itself.

The following scale can be used to determine the degree of alignment between a task and a standard:

Strong Alignment: The task clearly aligns to the standard; the task and the standard are almost one and the same; the task addresses all parts and honors the intent of the standard.

Moderate Alignment: The task addresses the standard; the standard is part of the task but is not the primary focus.

Weak Alignment: The task touches on the standard; the standard may occur but is not guaranteed to be part of the task.

A helpful activity, one that is useful in unpacking the scale and understanding alignment, is to rate the alignment of different tasks to a selected standard. Use the preceding scale to rate the degree of alignment between each task in Figure 2.1 and the following standard:

RI.11-12.7 Integrate and evaluate multiple sources of information presented in diverse formats and media (e.g., visually, quantitatively) as well as in words in order to address a question or solve a problem.

The first example in Figure 2.1, watching a video explaining the history of film, is weakly aligned to the standard; students are only viewing one source, without a specific purpose. The second example is a strongly

Figure 2.1
DEGREE OF ALIGNMENT

Task Description	Degree of Alignment
Students watch a video explaining the history of film.	*weak – not multiple sources*
Students read, watch, and analyze information and data to identify reasons for Latino immigration, challenges immigrants face, and immigrants' quality of life after arrival in the United States. They critique the origin of their sources to determine their reliability. Students use this information to write the introduction to a student-selected collection of memoirs, short stories, and poetry that illustrates the life of immigrants and answers the question *Can history be told through a story?*	*multiple sources diverse formats address a question* *strong*
Students use nonfiction text, videos, and quantitative data as part of their research to complete a paper on an event recounted in a historical novel of their choice.	*not addressing a question or solving a problem*

aligned task. Here students are reading, watching, and analyzing data, indicating the use of diverse media and formats—text, video, and charts and graphs. They evaluate the credibility of their sources as a means of determining the accuracy of their information. Students then use the information to answer the question *Can history be told through a story?* The last example is moderately aligned to the standard. It focuses on using a variety of sources, but it is unclear as to whether students are responding to a specific question or problem.

The goal is to ensure that the curriculum contains strongly aligned tasks. If we rely on the use of weakly aligned or moderately aligned tasks, students may not have the opportunity to engage in meaningful, relevant, and cognitively demanding tasks required by the school or district standards. A recent study by the Education Trust illustrates this situation. The study found that only 4 in 10 assignments (38 percent) were aligned with a grade-appropriate Common Core standard. As a result, students were often given short, less challenging tasks with a great deal of support that undermined the intention of the standards and lessened the required thinking (Brookins, Santelises, & Dabrowski, 2015). All students should have the opportunity to engage in cognitively demanding texts with scaffolds and supports dependent on need. A curriculum designed with this belief in mind allows teachers to make instructional decisions based on the needs of the students they are teaching. A quality curriculum designed with high-quality, strongly aligned tasks takes the first step in ensuring that this happens.

A task that is strongly aligned to a standard meets the following criteria:

1. The standard and the task are difficult to separate from each other.

2. The task requires students to fully engage in activities that align to all the skills embedded within the standard, usually requiring multiple steps.

3. The task reflects the intent of the standard.

Examine the standards and corresponding tasks in Figure 2.2. As you read through the tasks in Column 2, underline the part of the task description

Figure 2.2

TASK ALIGNMENT

thoughtfulness? (handwritten)

Standard	Task
Disposition of Practice: Commitment to Reflection • Willingness to devote time and energy to think about decisions, learning, and work in ways that promote thoughtfulness (Martin-Kniep, 2008). *verbs* (handwritten) *nouns* (handwritten)	Students investigate different ways in which young people can "make a difference." They find examples of community service, fundraisers, and organizations that have been led by young people and have made a difference in the lives of others. Students write a summary of each example they find and record their thoughts, questions, and connections. They work in small groups to determine a way they can make a difference. Students implement their plan and collect data during implementation, altering their plan as necessary. Students write a reflection on their experience and modify their plan in order to implement it again in the future.
• Students make connections by relating ideas *within* the content or *among* content areas and select or devise one approach among many alternatives on how a situation can be solved (Webb's Depth of Knowledge; Webb et al., 2005). *connections* (handwritten)	Students pursue the question *How healthy is the United States?* by documenting their own nutrition and exercise habits over a six-week period using a health-journal app. After documenting their own health, they conduct research that pursues questions such as these: • What are the nutritional and exercise habits of Americans in different age groups? • Are all the research findings regarding American health habits the same? How do they compare? • How does society reflect these health habits? • How do American health habits affect other areas of American life, such as economics and government? Students use their own experience to analyze the current state of American health. They write an evaluation of their own health in light of their findings, and prepare an action plan for pursuing a healthy life.

that reflects the standard in Column 1. By underlining the task in the examples, you can determine if the task meets the criteria for strong alignment.

In the first example, the multistep process of finding examples of community service, fundraisers, and organizations; writing a summary and recording thoughts, ideas, and questions; and creating, implementing, revising, and reflecting on a plan is evidence of the willingness to devote time and energy to thinking about decisions, learning, and work in ways that promote thoughtfulness. The alignment can therefore be considered strong.

In the second example, students document their own nutrition and exercise habits, conduct research, analyze the current state of American health, write an evaluation of their own health, and prepare an action plan for pursuing a healthy life. The task seamlessly intertwines health content with literacy skills, and it provides students with a personalized problem that could be solved in multiple ways, once again showing that when the task and standard are the same, alignment is strong.

Once you can recognize the degree of alignment between a task and a standard, it becomes possible to revise a task so it strongly aligns to a standard. Returning to Figure 2.1, we can revise the weakly aligned task (students watch a video explaining the history of film) to make it strong by expanding on the resources and focusing the research on a specific question. Now instead of watching a video explaining the history of film, students read and analyze multimedia resources, articles, and commentaries on the role of film in society, and they examine data regarding film development and usage. They consider the origin of the materials, noting the authors and website creators to determine the credibility of their sources. Students use this information to create a multimedia presentation in which they analyze a film of their choice and answer the question *Does film form or follow the norms and values of a society?*

We can also revise the moderately aligned task from Figure 2.1 for stronger alignment by adding a question to guide the reading of the different sources. In the original task, students are using nonfiction text, videos, and quantitative data to complete a paper on an event recounted in a historical novel of their choice. By adding the question *Does literature reflect life?* the research and the resulting paper have a specific purpose.

Content-Area Alignment

The same criteria apply to alignment in the content areas. However, alignment in the content areas often includes alignment to standards with different focuses. For example, consider the following task. Students read three articles to learn about different explanations of climate change, how it is caused, and the resulting impact of climate change on biodiversity. Students are asked to engage in this task in order to understand content identified in the Next Generation Science Standards (NGSS) and apply literacy skills to access the content, including those identified in Common Core standard RST.9-10.6:

> Analyze the author's purpose in providing an explanation, describing a procedure, or discussing an experiment in a text, defining the question the author seeks to address.

The task strongly aligns to the reading standard because it requires students to analyze the author's explanation of climate change. However, when we examine the task for alignment to the science standard, we see that it is actually weakly aligned.

The Next Generation Science Standards contain information about performance, science and engineering practices, disciplinary core ideas, and crosscutting concepts. For the sake of this example, let's work with one of the NGSS's performance expectations and a corresponding core idea related to the topic of Interdependent Relationships in the Ecosystem.

HS-LS4-6

> Create or revise a simulation to test a solution to mitigate adverse impacts of human activity on biodiversity. [Clarification Statement: Emphasis is on designing solutions for a proposed problem related to threatened or endangered species, or to genetic variation of organisms for multiple species.]

LS4.D: Biodiversity and Humans

Humans depend on the living world for the resources and other benefits provided by biodiversity. But human activity is also having adverse impacts on biodiversity through overpopulation, overexploitation, habitat destruction, pollution, introduction of invasive species, and climate change. . . . Thus sustaining biodiversity so that ecosystem functioning and productivity are maintained is essential to supporting and enhancing life on Earth. Sustaining biodiversity also aids humanity by preserving landscapes of recreational or inspirational value.

Exploring the different views on climate change is only one part of the core idea LS4.D: Biodiversity and Humans, which is why the task is weakly aligned. To strongly align to the core idea, students would also need to examine

- Speciation and extinction.
- Adverse impacts of human behavior, including overpopulation, overexploitation, habitat destruction, pollution, introduction of invasive species, and climate change.
- Biological extinction, because many species are unable to survive in changed environments and die out.
- The effects of biological extinction.
- The importance of sustaining biodiversity.
- Ways to sustain biodiversity.

One of the challenges related to strong alignment to content standards is making sure that all of the content included in the standard is also included in the curriculum, which may require more than one task. Addressing only one aspect of the content does not constitute alignment. For strong alignment to occur, the curriculum must include all the content in the standards.

By itself, the science core idea does not communicate how the students will acquire the information. This is why content standards are paired with literacy standards, as shown in the original example. Students are learning about climate change through reading. Their next learning experience may include a task that has them listening to a multimedia presentation to learn about the effects of biological distinction.

Alignment becomes even more complex as more standards are added. In this extension of the example, the core idea is presented with a performance expectation. Now for strong alignment to occur, students would need to formulate and test a possible solution for addressing the negative human impact on biodiversity. This undertaking could include

- Choosing an area of focus.
- Creating or revising a simulation that includes mathematical and computational thinking.
- Developing or evaluating a solution, taking into consideration cost, safety, reliability, and social, cultural, and environmental impacts.
- Using physical models and computers.
- Using empirical evidence to differentiate between cause and correlation and to make claims about specific causes and effects.

Now the original reading task serves a small role in a big picture. Regardless of scope, however, the concept of alignment remains the same. In the content areas, it means examining alignment in terms of content to be taught, content-specified skills such as the performance expectation, and the role of literacy in accessing and communicating the content.

Implications for Evaluating, Creating, or Revising Curriculum

Understanding that alignment occurs by degree rather than extremes is important to ensuring that students have opportunities to truly learn and practice the skills embedded in the standards. When evaluating curriculum, one way to check for strong alignment is to choose sample tasks from various units and determine the degree of alignment between the task and the standard identified using the scale of weak, moderate, and strong, as previously described. The tasks you choose to evaluate should represent those found in daily lessons, extended activities, and assessments. The chart in Figure 2.3 is a helpful tool for gathering and evaluating this information. An example at the top of the chart illustrates the process.

You can add additional rows to the chart based on the number of tasks you are examining. It is advantageous to analyze multiple tasks of different lengths and purposes. <u>Determining the degree of alignment is particularly important when examining published curriculum and instructional materials.</u> A report from the Brown Center on Education

Figure 2.3

DETERMINING ALIGNMENT IN A CURRICULUM

Task Description	Standard	Degree of Alignment	Notes for Revision
Students read several documents related to the events that occurred in Birmingham, Alabama, in 1963, including Dr. Martin Luther King's "Letter from Birmingham Jail" and a reprinted newspaper article from the *New York Times* in 1963. As they read the texts, they work with different-colored highlighters to show how the texts address the event in a similar fashion and any disconnect among the texts.	RI.9-10.9 <u>Analyze</u> seminal U.S. documents of historical and literary significance (e.g., Washington's Farewell Address, the Gettysburg Address, Roosevelt's Four Freedoms speech, King's "Letter from Birmingham Jail"), including how they address related themes and concepts.	Moderate	• Include an additional reading such as "Ballad of Birmingham" by Dudley Randall. • Provide opportunity for discussion on the ways the texts describe the same event, the reasons for the differences in their descriptions, and the impact on student understanding of the events of Birmingham as a result of reading the different accounts.
Task 1:			
Task 2:			

Policy at Brookings included this observation about publishing companies' initial responses to the Common Core State Standards: "Publishers of instructional materials are lining up to declare the alignment of their materials with the Common Core standards using the most superficial of definitions" (Chingos & Whitehurst, 2012, p. 1). Although publishers have made some improvements, those have not been enough; nor have they been consistent. Some companies have simply done a better job than others of aligning their materials, and with such inconsistencies, checking the degree of alignment is important.

Addressed, Taught, and Assessed: Three Ways to Look at Standards   *curriculum*

When examining curriculum, we are looking for tasks that are strongly aligned to the standards. What will help or hamper this determination is the way in which the curriculum communicates information about the standards and their value or emphasis.

We can view standards in different ways: those that are addressed, those that are taught, and those that are taught and assessed. Standards that are addressed are those that are touched upon but not necessarily the primary focus of a unit within a curriculum. Standards that are taught are those that involve students engaging in activities that practice the skills embedded within the standards. Standards that are taught and assessed are the standards that are the focus of instruction and are evaluated during the unit of study.

Let's examine a 4th grade unit to determine the difference between standards that are addressed and those that are taught and assessed. In this unit, students are examining the essential question *Is there more than one way to tell a story?* They are reading collections of texts that are connected by theme and that include stories from cultures other than the United States, nonfiction text, and dramas and stories that have been made into films. As they read, they take note of how the texts approach similar themes, and the similarities and differences between texts and their visual presentations. As a result of their examination, students write a proposal for a new movie based on a book of their choice.

The Common Core reading literature standards for this unit include the following:

RL.4.1   Refer to details and examples in a text when explaining what the text says explicitly and when drawing inferences from the text.

RL.4.2   Determine a theme of a story, drama, or poem from details in the text; summarize the text.

RL.4.3   Describe in depth a character, setting, or event in a story or drama, drawing on specific details in the text (e.g., a character's thoughts, words, or actions).

RL.4.5   Explain major differences between poems, drama, and prose, and refer to the structural elements of poems (e.g., verse, rhythm, meter) and drama (e.g., casts of characters, settings, descriptions, dialogue, stage directions) when writing or speaking about a text.

RL.4.6   Compare and contrast the point of view from which different stories are narrated, including the difference between first- and third-person narrations.

RL.4.7   Make connections between the text of a story or drama and a visual or oral presentation of the text, identifying where each version reflects specific descriptions and directions in the text.

RL.4.9   Compare and contrast the treatment of similar themes and topics (e.g., opposition of good and evil) and patterns of events (e.g., the quest) in stories, myths, and traditional literature from different cultures.

At first glance, it is easy to see why these standards were chosen; it is possible for students to use the skills that are embedded in all of these standards. However, potential does not mean the task is aligned, nor that the standard should be listed as a unit outcome. The question goes back to alignment and to what degree the tasks within the unit align to the standards. Based on this understanding, some of these standards are really just being addressed in the unit. The students are using the skills, but those skills are not the central focus of the unit. Further examination will reveal which standards are being addressed and which are being taught and assessed.

Throughout the unit, students read a variety of different text and film collections that may include the following:

- *The Invention of Hugo Cabret* by Brian Selznick, the film of the same title, and *Toys! Amazing Stories Behind Some Great Inventions* by Don Wulffson

- *The Lorax* by Dr. Seuss, the film of the same title, a nonfiction text on protecting the environment, and a folktale

- The poem "Little Red Riding Hood and the Wolf" by Roald Dahl, a picture book of Little Red Riding Hood, and *Lon Po Po: A Red-Riding Hood Story from China* by Ed Young

Students complete various activities and participate in discussions about the texts and films, referring to details and examples that support their thinking. These activities allow students to identify and examine common themes within the collections of texts, and to examine the unique structures of the different types of texts. They also provide students with the opportunity to generate criteria to use when comparing texts and their film versions.

At different points in the unit, students complete written responses in which they summarize the text and respond to the following questions, using specific evidence from the text:

- What is the theme of the story? How do the details in the text reveal the theme?

- How is the text structured? How does the structure affect the story?

- In what ways does the film reflect the descriptions and directions in the text?

- How do the text and the film differ? How do these differences affect the story?
  - How do the texts and films treat the same theme?

Given what we know about strong alignment, we can identify the standards that are taught and assessed when the task directions and the standards are placed next to each other, as in Figure 2.4. The standards that strongly align with the tasks—meaning the tasks and standard are difficult to separate from each other, and the intent of the standard remains intact—fall into either the category of "taught" or "taught and assessed." What is the difference? When a standard is taught, the task occurs during instruction. We see this in the 4th grade unit when students complete activities and participate in discussions. Students have the opportunity to practice the skills embedded in the standard with teacher guidance and feedback. When standards are taught and assessed, this still occurs, but there is also an assessment opportunity that allows the teacher to check and monitor student understanding. The reader-response journals serve this purpose in the 4th grade example.

Figure 2.4 shows which tasks and standards are aligned and also reveals that two of the standards identified are not aligned to a specific task in the unit:

- RL.4.3 Describe in depth a character, setting, or event in a story or drama, drawing on specific details in the text (e.g., a character's thoughts, words, or actions).

- RL.4.6 Compare and contrast the point of view from which different stories are narrated, including the difference between first- and third-person narrations.

Some may argue that students will need to describe the characters, setting, and events of the story when they use key details from the text to identify the theme. It is also possible for students to compare and contrast the point of view from which different stories are narrated by examining point of view in the different collections of stories. However, although these things may occur, the unit has not been designed with the explicit intent to allow students to practice these skills and the teacher to assess

Figure 2.4
ANALYZING TASKS

Standard	Tasks
RL.4.1 Refer to details and examples in a text when explaining what the text says explicitly and when drawing inferences from the text.	Students complete activities, participate in discussions, and respond to questions using details, examples, and evidence from text.
RL.4.2 Determine a theme of a story, drama, or poem from details in the text; summarize the text.	Students identify common themes Students summarize the text. Reader Response: What is the theme of the story? How do the details in the text reveal the theme?
RL.4.3 Describe in depth a character, setting, or event in a story or drama, drawing on specific details in the text (e.g., a character's thoughts, words, or actions).	
RL.4.5 Explain major differences between poems, drama, and prose, and refer to the structural elements of poems (e.g., verse, rhythm, meter) and drama (e.g., casts of characters, settings, descriptions, dialogue, stage directions) when writing or speaking about a text.	Students examine the unique structure of the different type of texts. Reader Response: How is the text structured? How does the structure affect the story?
RL.4.6 Compare and contrast the point of view from which different stories are narrated, including the difference between first- and third-person narrations.	
RL.4.7 Make connections between the text of a story or drama and a visual or oral presentation of the text, identifying where each version reflects specific descriptions and directions in the text.	Students identify criteria to use when comparing text and film. Reader Response: In what ways does the film reflect the descriptions and directions in the text? How does it differ? How do these differences affect the story?
RL.4.9 Compare and contrast the treatment of similar themes and topics (e.g., opposition of good and evil) and patterns of events (e.g., the quest) in stories, myths, and traditional literature from different cultures.	Students identify and examine common themes within the collections of texts. Reader Response: How do the texts in the collection treat the same theme?

them. We can consider these standards to be addressed only. The teacher may ask students to draw upon these skills or the skills may inadvertently occur, but they are not explicitly at the center of instruction and assessment in this unit.

Why is it important to distinguish between standards that are addressed, taught, and taught and assessed? Why not just include all the standards? One reason is practicality. The 4th grade example just presented describes in depth the reading literature portion of the unit. Students are also reading informational texts, writing, and speaking and listening within the unit. Including all standards from all areas would create a massive and unmanageable unit that could potentially go on for several months, therefore defeating the intent of organizing curriculum into units.

The other reason is focus. Educational researchers such as Rick Stiggins, W. James Popham, Robert Marzano, and Susan Brookhart have repeatedly discussed the impact of clear learning targets on students (Marzano, Pickering, & Pollock, 2001; Moss & Brookhart, 2012; Popham, 1999; Stiggins, 1997). Prioritizing the standards within units will help teachers to identify learning targets, share those targets with their students, and develop and use appropriate learning activities. Students will be aware of what they need to know and be able to do, have plenty of opportunities to practice the skills within the standards, and receive appropriate feedback and guidance from their teachers.

Prioritizing a set of standards in one unit is not done at the expense of other standards. When standards are carefully organized throughout the year, students will have the opportunity to practice the skills related to all standards, which is the focus of Chapter 3.

Taught and Assessed Standards in the Content Areas

The same concept of taught and assessed standards applies to the content areas as well. The difference, however, will depend on the specificity of the content-area standards or content understandings. In many cases, these standards or content understandings are vague and open to interpretation.

For example, consider the following content understandings from across the United States. According to the *Texas Essential Knowledge and Skills for Social Studies*, the student is expected to understand "the domestic and international impact of U.S. participation in World War II. The student is expected to identify reasons for U.S. involvement in World War II, including Italian, German, and Japanese dictatorships and their aggression, especially the attack on Pearl Harbor" (Texas Education Agency, 2010). In California, students are expected to "analyze America's participation in World War II. They examine the origins of American involvement in the war, with an emphasis on the events that precipitated the attack on Pearl Harbor" (California Academic Content Standards Commission [CACSC], 2000). In New York State, the following conceptual understandings describe what students need to know:

11.10   The United States participated in World War II as part of an Allied force to prevent military conquests by Germany, Italy, and Japan. United States policies during and immediately after World War II had a significant impact on American political, economic, and social life.

11.10.a   Multiple factors contributed to a rise in authoritarian forms of government and ideologies such as fascism, communism, and socialism after World War I.

11.10.b   The United States and the international community did not respond with force to aggressive German and Japanese actions that violated international treaties agreed to following World War I.

11.10.c   In the 1930s, public opinion slowly moved toward supporting a more active United States involvement in world affairs.

11.10.d   United States involvement moved from a policy of neutrality at the beginning of World War II and evolved into a pro-Allied position, culminating in direct and active United States involvement. (New York State, 2013)

Each of these documents provides information about what students should know about the United States entry into World War II, but none of them—regardless of the length of the description—offer specifics as to exactly what needs to be taught, what students need to be able to do with that knowledge, or how they can demonstrate that knowledge.

For the concept of taught and assessed to apply to these content standards, teachers first have to identify the "nonnegotiable." What exactly will students need to know, for example, about German, Italian, and Japanese aggression before the start of World War II? What should they know about the attack on Pearl Harbor? I have sat through many conversations in which teachers have discussed what they teach and what they do not teach in a unit of study, and there is rarely unanimous agreement. It is through these conversations, however, that teachers unpack the curriculum documents and identify the specifics about what needs to be taught and assessed.

Additional Implications for Evaluating, Creating, or Revising Curriculum

Certain indicators show that all the standards identified within the unit have been given equal weight. One is when all or most of the standards have been listed in a unit, as in the 4th grade example. Possibility does not indicate alignment. There need to be sufficient and focused practice and assessment opportunities within the unit for a standard to be considered taught and assessed. Including all standards in one unit does not allow for the necessary time to practice the embedded skills. Even with the identification of taught and assessed standards, standards will need to be revisited throughout the year to provide opportunities for reinforcement and attainment.

A second indication that careful thought has not been given to the identification of standards is when the standards identified in the overview or introduction to the unit are not the same as those identified in individual lessons. This mismatch suggests that the standards being taught are not necessarily those being assessed. Unfortunately, I have found this to be a common problem with textbooks and other learning materials.

So the following question arises: What do you do if you are working with a curriculum in which it is difficult to determine the focus standards? The task then becomes to prioritize the standards by clearly identifying and labeling those that are taught and assessed, and distinguishing them from those that are addressed. For existing or published curriculums, this may mean reviewing existing tasks to determine which standards are truly being taught and assessed. Although this effort may take some time, it is time well spent. Without such distinction, the unit will not be cohesive, and it will be very difficult to ensure that all users of the curriculum will understand the focus of instruction and assessment.

An additional strategy for ensuring that the standards identified are those that are taught and assessed is to actually code the standard into the document and create a unit blueprint. For example, if the original 4th grade document were coded with the standards, it would look like this:

> Throughout the unit, students read a variety of different text and film collections [RL.4.5, RL.4.9]. They complete different activities and participate in discussions about the texts and films, referring to details and examples that support their thinking [RL.4.1]. These activities allow students to identify and examine common themes [RL.4.2, RL.4.9] within the collections of texts, and examine the unique structures of the different types of texts, including folktales, stories, nonfiction, drama, and poems [RL.4.5]. They also provide students with the opportunity to identify criteria to use when comparing texts and their film versions [RL.4.7].
>
> At different points in the unit, students complete written responses in which they summarize the text [RL.4.2] and respond to the following questions, using specific evidence from the text [RL.4.1]:
>
> - What is the theme of the story? How do the details in the text reveal the theme? [RL.4.2]
> - How is the text structured? How does the structure affect the story? [RL.4.5]

- In what ways does the film reflect the descriptions and directions in the text? [RL.4.7]
- How do the text and the film differ? How do these differences affect the story? [RL.4.7]
- How do the texts or films treat the same theme? [RL.4.9]

A benefit to coding the standards as the unit is created is that it ensures that the tasks within the unit are strongly aligned and can be taught and assessed. Teachers can make decisions about the type of texts, activities, and assessments as they draft the unit. The process also reveals areas where alignment between a task and a standard is weak so that that area can be revised and made stronger, or when a standard selected for a unit early in the design process no longer makes sense and should be removed from the unit.

Summary: Alignment to Standards

Two critical areas to examine when evaluating or designing curriculum for standards alignment are (1) degree of alignment and (2) communication of standards that are taught and assessed. Although curriculum documents may claim alignment, the degree to which the curriculum is aligned may vary. Tasks can be weakly, moderately, or strongly aligned to standards. A quality curriculum will ensure strong alignment, meaning the tasks and standard are difficult to distinguish from each other and the intent of the standard remains intact.

Listing a standard in a unit of study is not enough to claim that it is sufficiently emphasized throughout the unit. Standards that are addressed, taught, and taught and assessed may all be included in one unit. A high-quality curriculum document will communicate the difference between these standards or include only those that are taught and assessed, allowing teachers to make purposeful decisions about what to teach and how to teach it and to share learning targets with their students. Students should be given the opportunity to practice the skills embedded in the standards and receive guidance and feedback from their teachers before being assessed.

Understanding degree of alignment can help educators identify those tasks in need of revision and revise them to increase the degree of alignment between the task and the standards. In addition, it can help them to analyze the standards to reveal those that are taught and assessed, as well as those that are simply addressed. The coding of standards will ensure both alignment and the inclusion of standards that are taught and assessed in a unit of study.

Tools and Activities for Evaluation, Design, and Revision

- **Degree of Alignment**—This activity is helpful in establishing a common understanding of the degree of alignment between tasks and standards (see Figure 2.1 for an example). With this understanding, educators can evaluate tasks in an existing curriculum to determine their degree of alignment and, when necessary, revise them so they strongly align to the standards. Educators can also use this understanding to design strongly aligned tasks.

- **Analyzing Tasks for Strong Alignment**—This activity allows educators to see the connection between what students are asked to do and the standard itself (see Figure 2.2 for an example). It is helpful in clarifying the criteria for a strongly aligned task.

- **Determining Alignment in a Curriculum**—A chart like the one in Figure 2.3 can be used for sampling tasks within a curriculum to ensure that they are strongly aligned and revise those that are not.

- **Coding Standards**—Coding of standards into tasks ensures strong alignment and identifies weakly or moderately aligned tasks in need of revision (see example on pp. 43–44).

Checklist for Evaluation, Design, and Revision

☐ The tasks are strongly aligned to the standards. It is difficult to distinguish between the task and the standard, all skills identified in the standard are included in the task, and the task honors the intent of the standard.

☐ The standards that are *taught and assessed* are clearly identified and distinguished from those that are *addressed*.

Standards Placement and Emphasis

In Chapter 2 we explored the degree of alignment between standards and tasks, and the need to focus a unit of study on a set of specific standards that are taught and assessed within that unit. An individual task is one of many that lie inside a larger unit of study, and a unit is only part of a bigger curriculum made up of several more units. In evaluating or creating a curriculum, it is important not only to examine the alignment of tasks to standards within a unit, but also to examine the placement and sequencing of standards over the entire curriculum.

Let's look at the 7th grade example from Chapter 2 to illustrate the nesting of tasks within units, and units within a yearly curriculum. The 7th graders examined several sonnets to determine how they differed from other types of poetry and then focused specifically on the sonnet "How do I love thee? Let me count the ways" to examine how the structure of a sonnet affects the poem's message. This task strongly aligns to one standard and is one of many tasks that students will complete as they engage in a unit of study called The Power of Language. In this unit, students will examine not only poetry but also speeches, plays, and editorials in order to determine how the author's use of language and structure affects his or her ability to tell a story, convey a message, or create an argument. As a result of their study and additional research on a topic of their choice, students will select an appropriate format in which to convey their own message, thoughts, or argument.

Although the task focuses on one standard, the unit focuses on a specific set of standards that will be taught and assessed within the unit. Those standards that are not taught and assessed in the Power of Language unit will be emphasized in other units. The Power of Language is only one piece of a puzzle, and like each piece of a puzzle, it needs to be assembled into a cohesive whole.

A quality curriculum will purposefully emphasize and place standards within specific units. As you examine an existing curriculum or design your own, it is important to make sure that all standards are taught and assessed, and to understand why specific standards fit inside each unit and how units build from one to another.

Standards Analysis: Determining Emphasis and Placement

One of the most unique places where I have worked is the Fire Island School District in New York. Fire Island is a small district located on the barrier beach of Long Island. Each year I have worked with the district's superintendent, Loretta Ferraro, to design a professional development program that examined best practices in instruction and assessment and was tailored to meet the needs of the school. When New York State adopted the Common Core Learning Standards, teachers in the district—Gabrielle Donovan, Shannon Picinich, Karen McNulty, and Jeanene Crawson—began to create and align their units of study. As they worked on their curriculum, they incorporated the practices we explored and explicitly aligned student tasks to the standards.

In the revision stage of the work, the teachers used a standards-analysis document to examine the placement and emphasis of standards within the curriculum. There are different versions of the standards-analysis document. The two models presented here reference the Common Core State Standards but can be adapted to any set of standards.

The standards-analysis document shown in Figure 3.1, developed by Learner-Centered Initiatives consultant Dr. Liz Locatelli, allows the user to read and see the relationship between the units of study and the specific standards that are taught and assessed in that unit. Each standard is fully written out, and columns provide space for noting where the standard has been included in the units of study. This standards-analysis document is especially helpful when planning a curriculum or documenting the placement of standards as the curriculum is being developed.

The standards-analysis document in Figure 3.2 (see p. 50) shows the same relationships but condenses the data. Users simply put the unit numbers in the spaces related to the appropriate standard. This document is particularly useful for analyzing a curriculum to make revisions, or it can be used as a quick reference tool when designing units of study.

In Fire Island we worked with the second document because we wanted to gather and analyze data from existing units of study. Figure 3.3 (see p. 51) represents what we found as a result of identifying the location of standards taught and assessed in the 5th and 6th grade curriculum.

At first glance, the chart looks like a random collection of numbers, but careful analysis is quite revealing. We used the following questions to guide us through the analysis process:

- What standards are emphasized? Why?
- Where are there gaps or standards that are underemphasized? Why?
- What additional questions do the data generate?
- What revisions need to be made to create a balanced and spiraled curriculum?

Here is what we discovered: certain standards were identified as taught and assessed in every unit or almost every unit. Discussion with the 5th and 6th grade teacher, Mrs. Gabrielle Donovan, revealed that this was not done intentionally but did reflect what she reinforced with her

Figure 3.1
STANDARDS-ANALYSIS DOCUMENT 1

Reading Literature	Unit 1	Unit 2	Unit 3	Unit 4	Unit 5	Unit 6
RL.5.1 Quote accurately from a text when explaining what the text says explicitly and when drawing inferences from the text.						
RL.5.2 Determine a theme of a story, drama, or poem from details in the text, including how characters in a story or drama respond to challenges or how the speaker in a poem reflects upon a topic; summarize the text.						
RL.5.3 Compare and contrast two or more characters, settings, or events in a story or drama, drawing on specific details in the text (e.g., how characters interact).						
RL.5.4 Determine the meaning of words and phrases as they are used in a text, including figurative language such as metaphors and similes.						
RL.5.5 Explain how a series of chapters, scenes, or stanzas fits together to provide the overall structure of a particular story, drama, or poem.						
RL.5.6 Describe how a narrator's or speaker's point of view influences how events are described.						
RL.5.7 Analyze how visual and multimedia elements contribute to the meaning, tone, or beauty of a text (e.g., graphic novel, multimedia presentation of fiction, folktale, myth, poem).						
(RL.5.8 not applicable to literature)						
RL.5.9 Compare and contrast stories in the same genre (e.g., mysteries and adventure stories) on their approaches to similar themes and topics.						

Source: © 2013 by Learner-Centered Initiatives. Used with permission.

Figure 3.2

STANDARDS-ANALYSIS DOCUMENT 2

Standard	Reading Literature	Reading Information	Writing	Speaking and Listening	Language	Strand
1						
2						
3						
4	Numbers represent the grade-level standard. The maximum number of standards found in a given strand of the CCSS is 10. Not all strands have 10 standards. An X indicates that the standard does not exist.					
5						
6						
7				X	X	
8	X			X	X	
9				X	X	
10				X	X	

Source: © 2012 by Learner-Centered Initiatives. Used with permission.

students in class. For example, Mrs. Donovan emphasized the first standard in reading literature and reading information:

> RL.6.1 and RI.6.1   Cite textual evidence to support analysis of what the text says explicitly as well as inferences drawn from the text.

Mrs. Donovan shared with her students the importance of backing up their statements with evidence from the text and had taught them strategies for doing so. As a result, they were expected to use textual evidence during discussions and when writing.

Other standards identified as being emphasized, such as Writing Standard 2, were not reflective of actual practice:

Figure 3.3

COMPLETED STANDARDS-ANALYSIS DOCUMENT

Standard	Reading Literature	Reading Information	Writing	Speaking and Listening	Language
1	1, 2, 3, 5, 6	1, 2, 3, 4, 6	1, 2, 6	1, 2, 3, 5, 6	1, 2
2	1, 2, 3, 5, 6	1, 2, 3, 4, 6	1, 2, 3, 5	2	
3	1, 2, 3	1, 2, 6	2, 3	1, 2, 5	
4	1, 2, 3, 5	1, 2	1, 2, 3	1, 3, 5	1
5	5	2, 6	2, 5	1, 3, 5	
6	5, 6	1	1	1, 3, 5	
7	3, 5	1, 2, 3, 4, 6	1, 2, 3, 6	X	X
8	X	2, 4, 6	1, 2, 3, 6	X	X
9	2, 3, 5	1, 2, 3, 4, 6	1, 2, 3, 6	X	X
10			1, 2, 3	X	X
11	1, 3, 5	X	3, 5	X	X

Note:
- X indicates that there is no standard with that number.
- A blank space means the standard could not be found in a unit of study.
- New York State has 11 English language arts standards.

W.6.2   Write informative/explanatory texts to examine a topic and convey ideas, concepts, and information through the selection, organization, and analysis of relevant content.

a. Introduce a topic; organize ideas, concepts, and information, using strategies such as definition, classification, comparison/contrast, and cause/effect; include formatting (e.g., headings), graphics (e.g., charts, tables), and multimedia when useful to aiding comprehension.

b. Develop the topic with relevant facts, definitions, concrete details, quotations, or other information and examples.

c. Use appropriate transitions to clarify the relationships among ideas and concepts.

d. Use precise language and domain-specific vocabulary to inform about or explain the topic.

e. Establish and maintain a formal style.

f. Provide a concluding statement or section that follows from the information or explanation presented.

Mrs. Donovan shared that although students were often asked to write short informational pieces, those were mostly responses to text and not fully developed pieces that incorporated all the components of Standard 2. The standard was not taught and assessed as it was being represented in the standards-analysis document, and it needed to be removed from some of the units in order to accurately represent classroom practice.

Examination of the standards-analysis document revealed gaps and standards that were underemphasized. Some of the gaps were easily explained—for example, Standard 10 for reading literature and information:

RL.6.10 and RI.6.10   By the end of the year, read and comprehend literature, including stories, dramas, and poems, in the grades 6–8 text complexity band proficiently, with scaffolding as needed at the high end of the range.

Mrs. Donovan's students read different texts for different purposes on a daily basis, and because it was common practice, she had not included the standard in the units.

However, this was not the case with all of the standards that were identified as underemphasized. Closer examination revealed that some of the standards that had been included in only one or two units needed to be taught and assessed more consistently. For example, Mrs. Donovan recognized the importance of Standard 5:

> RL.6.5   Analyze how a particular sentence, chapter, scene, or stanza fits into the overall structure of a text and contributes to the development of the theme, setting, or plot.

Structure had not been explicitly targeted in the previous set of standards used by New York State, so this standard would require a more intentional change in practice.

After they had examined the standards-analysis document, several questions emerged for the Fire Island teachers about the placement and emphasis of standards in curriculum. These included the following:

- Is it necessary for all standards to be taught and assessed?
- Can certain standards be emphasized in all units? If so, how; or should those standards be included in the listing of the standards?
- How should standards be placed over the course of the year?
- What revisions need to be made to create a balanced and spiraled curriculum?

These questions are important to all curriculum, so we will examine them not only as they relate to the examples from the Fire Island School District but also in terms of their implications for other grade levels and content areas.

Is it necessary for all standards to be taught and assessed? The answer to this question is simple: yes. The standards you adopt or create articulate what you value. Picking and choosing standards based on preference does not honor the overall intent of the standards. Working with only some of the standards would make it quite easy to disregard the ones that you don't like, that are difficult to teach, or that fall outside your comfort zone. The result could be a curriculum that does not provide students with the opportunity to engage in rigorous tasks and, in the absence of ensuring that all standards have been included, would decrease the likelihood that students have engaged in learning activities that serve as foundations for subsequent years.

As discussed in Chapter 2, the standards identified in a unit of study should be those that are taught and assessed in the unit of study. By the end of the year, all standards should be taught and assessed, and ideally more than once so students have ample opportunity to practice and obtain the skills embedded in the standards.

Can certain standards be emphasized in all units? If so, how; or should those standards be included in the listing of the standards? Once again the answer to this question is yes, it is possible that certain standards can be emphasized in all units, particularly if the selected standard represents the intent behind the standards as a whole. However, this does not mean that the standard is equally emphasized in all units, nor that it should be listed in all units. Let's take a look at two different sets of standards to illustrate this.

Mrs. Donovan's rationale for the choice of Standard 1 validated the inclusion of that standard in all units. It was also supported by the intent of the Common Core State Standards, which was to shift practice in six areas (EngageNY, n.d.):

1. Balance of Informational and Literary Texts: Students read a variety of informational and literary texts that are complementary to one another.

2. Knowledge Across Disciplines: Students read and write as an integral part of learning in the content areas.

3. Staircase of Complexity: Students read increasingly complex text.

4. Textual Evidence: Students use specific evidence from the text when making an argument or sharing information.

5. Writing from Sources: Students write for different purposes: to argue, inform, or share.

6. Vocabulary: Students learn and incorporate academic and domain-specific vocabulary.

Because Standard 1 asks students to cite the text, it clearly supports the shift "Textual Evidence," so it made sense to include it in all units. But what did this mean for other standards? Mrs. Donovan had decided not to include Standard 10 in all units even though she asked students to read a variety of texts. This standard supports the shift "Staircase of Complexity." Why wouldn't the same thinking apply to this standard?

Clearly, there is no one right answer; both points make sense. However, the key behind all decisions regarding curriculum design is consistency, and this was surely not consistent practice. After some discussion, this is what was decided: The standard would be listed as taught and assessed when specific strategies for achieving the standard would be taught to the students. When the standard was not listed, students would still be expected to use the skills embedded in the standard.

Another example of choosing standards based on intent can be seen in the Next Generation Science Standards. Again, these standards represent conceptual shifts in practice, as explained in Appendix A of the Next Generation Science Standards (NGSS, n.d.) and paraphrased here:

1. Interconnected Nature of Science in the Real World: Science incorporates science and engineering practices, crosscutting concepts, and core ideas.

2. Performance Expectations: The standards identify what students need to be able to do but not necessarily the specifics of what they need to know.

3. Coherent Building of Science Concepts: There is a progression of knowledge that occurs over several years that leads to an overall understanding of science concepts by the end of high school. Each grade-level band builds off the previous band.

4. Deeper Understanding and Application of Content: The focus is on big ideas, not isolated facts.

5. Integration of Science and Engineering: Engineering and technology are given the same attention as scientific inquiry and used to help students apply science to their everyday lives.

6. College, Career, and Citizenship: Science is an integral part of daily life, and science knowledge will prepare students for making sense of their world.

7. Connection to the Common Core State Standards: There are many overlaps between the CCSS and the NGSS, showing the integral nature of the disciplines: science, English language arts, mathematics, and technology.

Honoring the shifts in science means ensuring that each unit incorporates standards representing science and engineering practices, crosscutting concepts, and core ideas, as well as the appropriate English language arts and literacy standards, and the standards for mathematics. The following high school example illustrates this practice.

Students choose a form of wave technology such as solar cells converting light into energy, medical imaging, or computer technology. They conduct research on how the wave technology works, who uses it and why, how it improves the quality of life, and how it is an improvement over past technology. Students create a display for a school-sponsored technology fair in which they share their research with the community and promote the use of current technology. Students include a model and a visual diagram showing how the technology works and a brochure for visitors to take with them.

In this unit of study, the following performance indicator (along with its related science and engineering practice, disciplinary core idea, and crosscutting concepts) is taught and assessed:

HS-PS4-5   Communicate technical information about how some technological devices use the principles of wave behavior and wave interactions with matter to transmit and capture information and energy.

In addition, the following Common Core standards for science are also assessed:

RST.11-12.7   Integrate and evaluate multiple sources of information presented in diverse formats and media (e.g., quantitative data, video, multimedia) in order to address a question or solve a problem.

WHST.11-12.2   Write informative/explanatory texts, including the narration of historical events, scientific procedures/experiments, or technical processes.

By including these standards, the unit is illustrating the science shift in practice "Connection to Common Core State Standards" in English language arts. An integral relationship connects the standards in English language arts and science, therefore honoring the intent of the standards.

How should standards be placed over the course of the year? For the teachers on Fire Island, this question arose as a result of the other two: if all standards should be taught and assessed and strategically placed within units of study, how do you know where they should be placed? This time, however, the answer was not so simple. Certain factors that should be considered in the placement of the standards through the curriculum include developmentally appropriate practice, gradual release of responsibility, grade-level focus skills, and outside forces such as state and national tests.

Developmentally appropriate practice. It is easy to lose sight of the fact that when we are discussing standards, we are talking about children, and developmental factors should be considered when determining or evaluating the placement of standards within a curriculum. For example, writing in kindergarten does not necessarily begin with print. Students progress from using marks, to drawing and using random letters, to using letters that represent sounds and words, to eventually using conventional print—and not necessarily in that order and at the same pace. Many kindergarten teachers agree that the best way for students to learn how to write is to begin by writing about themselves. Therefore, it would make sense that the first unit in a kindergarten classroom would include the standards for narrative writing and that these standards would be revisited later in the year when students have more experience as writers.

This idea also applies to what we understand about students as learners. Middle school students are undergoing great changes in their ability to think. Brain research has shown that they are moving from concrete to abstract thinking and to the beginnings of metacognition. They are developing skills in deductive reasoning, problem solving, and generalizing, which are manifested in such behaviors as maintaining strong, intense interests; preferring to interact with peers; and engaging in active learning (Lorain, 2015). With this in mind, it makes sense to include speaking and listening standards to teach students how to positively interact and learn from one another right from the beginning of the year.

Gradual release of responsibility. Standards are written in terms of what students should know and be able to do by the end of the year. For students to have ample opportunity to practice and then achieve the skills embedded in the standards, the standards should be consistently revisited throughout the year. The caution here is to make sure that the same standards are not always clustered together or that standards are not front- or back-loaded into the curriculum. In the Fire Island standards-analysis document (Figure 3.3), for example, Standard 6 for reading literature could be found only in Units 5 and 6, the last units of the year. This standard includes valuable skills:

> RL.6.6   Explain how an author develops the point of view of the narrator or speaker in a text.

There could be several explanations for why the standard was placed at the end of the year. Explaining how point of view influences how events are described and how the author develops point of view are much more difficult skills than simply identifying point of view. The teacher may not have realized that the standard went beyond identifying point of view, or he or she may have felt the students were not ready to apply their understanding of point of view. Regardless of whether the placement was purposeful or not, waiting until the end of the year is not advantageous to the students; they certainly will not have enough practice with a complex skill.

It is important to note here that each discipline presents subtle differences in its approach to standards. It is possible, then, that certain content-specific standards may be included in the curriculum only once if they are specific to a concept or topic. However, all standards from the content area should be taught and assessed by the end of the year, and those that transcend content should be strategically placed so students have opportunities to practice the embedded skills.

Grade-level focus skills. Careful analysis of standards documents will reveal if there are skills that should be emphasized in a curriculum for a particular grade level. The Common Core State Standards are a good example of this. The CCSS were written "backward" from the College and Career Readiness Anchor Standard to kindergarten so that the skills are scaffolded and students will be college- and career-ready upon graduation. By comparing a grade-level standard with the standards from the previous and following grade levels, you can identify emphasized grade-level skills, as seen in the 2nd grade example in Figure 3.4.

Students in 2nd grade are expected to be able to answer *who, what, where, when, why,* and *how* questions. Although they may have already done so in kindergarten and 1st grade and will continue to do so throughout their educational career, the CCSS has identified this as a focus for instruction in 2nd grade. It is the only grade level in which this particular skill has been explicitly identified. Figure 3.4 illustrates this emphasis through its coding:

- Bold, italicized print identifies language in the standard that is new to a grade level when it is compared to the previous grade level. This indicates the introduction of a new skill.

Figure 3.4
SCAFFOLDED STANDARDS

1st Grade	2nd Grade	3rd Grade
RL.1.1 Ask and answer questions about key details in a text.	RL.2.1 Ask and answer such questions as **_who, what, where, when, why, and how_** to demonstrate understanding of key details in a text.	RL.3.1 Ask and answer questions to demonstrate understanding of a text, **_referring explicitly to the text as the basis for the answers._**

must be over-learned

- Underlined print indicates language in the standard that is no longer part of the standard in the following grade level. This means that the skill is a necessary foundation for the following grade level.

- Print that is bold, italicized, and underlined indicates a skill that is specific to a grade level, as shown in the 2nd grade example.

The process of comparing grade-level standards to those that precede and follow is a valuable activity for teachers to engage in before designing or evaluating curriculum. It allows them to see the role of the grade-level curriculum in the big picture of curriculum. Understanding the skills that are introduced, reinforced, or mastered also provides insight into the placement of standards, as well as the type of instructional strategies that should be used for teaching them.

Other standards and content documents will convey information regarding learning progressions in a similar fashion. For example, Figure 3.5 is an excerpt from Appendix F of the Next Generation Science Standards, showing progressions of Science Practice 3: Planning and Carrying Out Investigations.

Once again, the coding of the standards (through boldface, italics, and underlining) reveals skills that are the focus of instruction because they are unique to a grade-level band. In this science example, the change in emphasis at each grade-level band is on the type of data collected and analyzed. The curriculum should therefore emphasize the different types of data as students engage in scientific investigations at the different band levels.

Outside forces, such as state and national tests. Another consideration in the placement of standards is the timing of state or national tests. If one of the goals of the curriculum is to avoid ongoing test prep or the dreaded test-prep unit, it is important to make sure that the standards that tend to be the focus of the standardized assessments are embedded in the curriculum before the actual exam. For example, the New York State ELA exam emphasizes a form of argumentative and informational writing; therefore, the corresponding writing standards should be the focus of instruction before the tests are administered so that students are

Figure 3.5

EXCERPTS FROM SCIENCE STANDARDS FOR PLANNING AND CARRYING OUT INVESTIGATIONS

Grades K–2	Grades 3–5	Grades 6–8	Grades 9–12
Planning and carrying out investigations to answer questions or test solutions to problems in K–2 builds on prior experiences and progresses to <u>simple</u> investigations, based on ***fair tests, which provide data*** to support explanations or design solutions.	Planning and carrying out investigations to answer questions or test solutions to problems in 3–5 builds on K–2 experiences and progresses to include investigations ***that control variables and provide evidence*** to support explanations or design solutions.	Planning and carrying out investigations in 6–8 builds on K–5 experiences and progresses to include investigations that use ***multiple variables*** and provide evidence to support explanations or solutions.	Planning and carrying out investigations in 9–12 builds on K–8 experiences and progresses to include investigations that provide evidence for and ***test conceptual, mathematical, physical, and empirical models.***
• With guidance, <u>plan and conduct an investigation in collaboration with peers (for K).</u>	• Plan and conduct an investigation collaboratively to produce data to serve as the basis for evidence, ***using fair tests in which variables are controlled and the number of trials considered.***	• Plan an investigation ***individually*** and collaboratively, ***and in the design: identify independent and dependent variables and controls, what tools are needed to do the gathering, how measurements will be recorded, and how many data are needed to support a claim.***	• Plan an investigation ***or test a design*** individually and collaboratively to ***produce data to serve as the basis for evidence as part of building and revising models, supporting explanations for phenomena, or testing solutions to problems. Consider possible confounding variables or effects and evaluate the investigation's design to ensure variables are controlled.***
• Plan and conduct an investigation collaboratively to ***produce data to serve as the basis for evidence to answer*** <u>a question.</u>			

Source: Next Generation Science Standards, Appendix F. Boldface, italics, and underlining do not appear in original.

prepared, but in a more natural way that is embedded in the curriculum rather than separate from it.

Putting It All Together

After exploring the answers to the three questions just discussed as they pertained to the Fire Island School District, it was time to answer the remaining analysis question: *What revisions need to be made to create a balanced and spiraled curriculum?* It was evident that all standards needed to be identified in the units where they were taught and assessed, placement of standards needed to support the shifts in practice and the big picture of curriculum, and standards needed strategic placement to ensure opportunities for review and attainment.

As a result of the standards analysis, Fire Island revised the placement of the standards in the curriculum, as shown in Figure 3.6. The revised standards-analysis document shows the following changes:

- All of the standards are taught and assessed throughout the year.

- Standards are placed in the curriculum strategically so that those that support the intent of the standards—in this case, the shifts in practice—are introduced early on and revisited throughout the year. For example, Standard 4 is included in the curriculum in Unit 1 for both reading literature and reading information:

RL.6.4   Determine the meaning of words and phrases as they are used in a text, including figurative and connotative meanings; analyze the impact of a specific word choice on meaning and tone.

RI.6.4   Determine the meaning of words and phrases as they are used in a text, including figurative, connotative, and technical meanings.

The CCSS emphasizes students' acquisition and integration of vocabulary into their expressive language. To accomplish this, students need to be taught very specific strategies. Including this standard in the first unit is one way to ensure that students have the time to practice and apply the

Figure 3.6
REVISED STANDARDS-ANALYSIS DOCUMENT

Standard	Reading Literature	Reading Information	Writing	Speaking and Listening	Language				
					a.	b.	c.	d.	e.
1	1, 3, 4	1, 3, 4	2, 4	1, 2, 3, 4, 5	1, 3	3, 6	2, 5	2, 5	1, 3
2	2, 3, 5	1, 2, 5	1, 5	1, 2, 5	1, 4	2, 4	2, 4	1, 3	1,3, 5
3	1, 2, 4	2, 4, 6	3, 6	4, 6	2, 3	3, 5	X	X	X
4	1, 3	1, 3	1, 3, 5	1, 4, 6	1, 4	2, 4	1, 3	X	X
5	2, 3, 5	2, 3, 5	1, 3, 5	1, 3, 6	1, 3	2, 3	2, 4	X	X
6	2, 4, 6	1, 4	1, 3, 6	1, 3, 6	2, 3				
7	3, 5	1, 2, 5	1, 2, 4, 6	X	X				
8	X	4, 6	4, 5	X	X				
9	2, 3, 6	3, 5	3	X	X				
10	1	1	1	X	X				
11	1, 3, 5	X	3, 5	X	X				

skills for learning and using new vocabulary throughout the year. The strategies they have been taught are revisited, and additional strategies are taught to the students in subsequent units.

- Standards that lay the foundation for other standards are included in the first unit. For example, the skills embedded in Reading Information Standard 2 include determining "a central idea of a text and how it is conveyed through particular details," and providing "a summary of the text distinct from personal opinions or judgments." These skills serve as the foundation for reading and analyzing informational text and therefore were included in Unit 1.

- All standards are revisited throughout the year. Conscious effort was made to ensure that there was no back- or front-loading of standards, and that the same standards were not always clustered together. Revisiting standards throughout the year provides an opportunity for students to practice the skills embedded in the standards and become proficient in using them independently.

Fire Island's story is actually quite typical of what happens in many schools. The situation is not so much that educators are reluctant to examine or determine the placement of standards as that placement and emphasis of standards are not a conscious and deliberate part of the process of curriculum evaluation or design. In Fire Island, the placement of standards occurred as individual units were developed and was often based on the topics and strategies under examination during professional development. In cases in which a district purchases a text or series as the curriculum, it may assume that the placement of standards has been carefully planned. The lesson to be learned from the Fire Island experience is that placement and emphasis of standards should be a conscious part of the curriculum design and evaluation process.

Summary: Standards Placement and Emphasis

There are many factors to consider when examining or deciding the placement and emphasis of standards within a curriculum. Some of the most important are the following:

- Although a unit may address many standards, only those that are being emphasized—meaning those that will guide the specific skills that will be taught and then assessed—should be listed. By the end of the year, all standards should be taught and assessed within the curriculum, ideally providing students with multiple opportunities to practice the skills embedded in the standards.

- Placement of standards throughout the year should be influenced by factors such as the overall intent of the standards, grade-level focus standards, gradual release of responsibility, and developmentally appropriate practice.

Tools and Activities for Evaluation, Design, and Revision

- **Standards-Analysis Documents** (Figures 3.1 and 3.2)—Two standards-analysis tools are available to help you both plan and analyze the placement of standards within the curriculum. Once you have collected the data, you can review these documents using the guiding questions provided in this chapter to determine if the placement and emphasis of standards reflect the overall intent of the standards, grade-level focus standards, gradual release of responsibility, and developmentally appropriate practice.

- **Determining Focus Standards**—This activity consists of coding (with boldface, italics, and underlining) standards to determine grade-level or grade-band emphasis. When teachers engage in this process, they not only determine what skills to emphasize but also become more familiar with cross-grade-level connections in the curriculum.

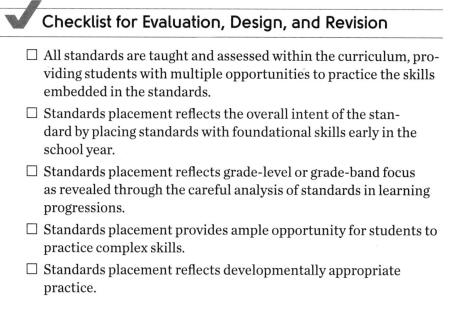

Checklist for Evaluation, Design, and Revision

☐ All standards are taught and assessed within the curriculum, providing students with multiple opportunities to practice the skills embedded in the standards.

☐ Standards placement reflects the overall intent of the standard by placing standards with foundational skills early in the school year.

☐ Standards placement reflects grade-level or grade-band focus as revealed through the careful analysis of standards in learning progressions.

☐ Standards placement provides ample opportunity for students to practice complex skills.

☐ Standards placement reflects developmentally appropriate practice.

Assessment Types and Purposes

In an "Assessment Manifesto" published in 2008, Rick Stiggins had this to say about assessments:

> If assessments are to support improvements in student learning, their results must inform students how to do better the next time. This will require communication of results that transmit sufficient understandable detail to guide the learner's actions. In such contexts, single scores or grades will not suffice.
>
> Further, to support learning, assessments must evolve from being *isolated occasional events attached to the end of teaching* to becoming *an ongoing series of interrelated events that reveal changes in student learning over time.* Such evidence will reveal to the learner and the teacher not only current achievement status, but also improvements in the student's capabilities—a powerful booster of confidence and motivation.
>
> Finally, to support learning, assessments must move beyond merely informing the instructional decisions of teachers and school leaders to informing decisions made by students, too. In the future, balanced assessment systems will need to be designed to *serve diverse purposes* by meeting the information needs of all decision makers. Historically, they have not done this. (2008, p. 3)

Stiggins's vision for assessment is one that I would hope all schools would want—assessments that support learning. However, as Stiggins also notes, this is not the case in all schools. Many schools view assessments as isolated events that students have no control over and that are used to generate a score and to separate those who are successful from those who are not. There is much more to assessment than that.

Understanding the roles of different types of assessments and the purposes they serve is the first step to developing or evaluating quality assessments in a curriculum. The second step is to develop or ensure the inclusion of high-quality, curriculum-embedded performance assessments—that is, assessments that produce, support, and then measure student learning (the focus of Chapter 5).

Types of Assessment

Assessment is defined as the strategic collection of evidence of student learning throughout the learning process (Martin-Kniep, 2006). Assessment does not automatically mean "test," although many people make that immediate association when hearing the word. Unfortunately, when standardized state tests became the norm in the mid-'90s, they were introduced as assessments, and the term *assessment* became equated with the word *test*. In actuality, tests are really one type of assessment. They fall under the category of *information-recall assessments*. Information-recall assessments include test formats such as multiple choice, true-false, matching columns, and short answers that require students to identify or provide the correct answer as deemed by the test creator.

Other types of assessments used in the classroom are *product assessments*, *demonstrations or performance assessments*, and *process assessments*. Product assessments result in the creation of a tangible product. They range from the very informal, such as sticky notes used to capture student thinking as they read, to formal research papers or essays. Demonstrations, sometimes called performance assessments, require students to do something and include behaviors observable by the teacher. Examples include informal small-group discussions, formal classroom debates, and individual and group presentations. A process assessment comes in the form of a product or demonstration but focuses on metacognition, asking students to reflect on their thinking and processes. A process assessment includes students' self-reflections, in which they answer questions such as *What did you find easy or difficult about this assessment?* and *What would you do differently?* This type also includes process journals in which students document steps in their research, as well as "Dear Reader" letters in which students explain the choice of work included in their portfolios and what it demonstrates about them as learners.

Combining Assessment Types

In some cases an assessment may include different types. For example, a test might contain information recall and a product—in other words, multiple-choice questions and an essay. A demonstration may include a product—for example, a presentation explaining a model.

It is also possible that a performance assessment such as a lab experiment might occur under testing conditions, and a short-answer test might be completed in small groups with access to resources. So another factor in considering the type of assessment is the conditions under which the assessment is implemented—on-demand or curriculum embedded. On-demand tasks are those that are separate from the curriculum. They require students to stop what they are doing in order to complete the assessment. Curriculum-embedded assessments are those that are integrated into daily instruction; they produce, as well as measure, learning (and they are explored in detail in Chapter 5).

When to Use Different Types of Assessments

Teachers recognize the different types of assessments in their practice, so the question is not whether they exist but rather when they should be used. The answer is, it depends on what you are assessing. Different types of standards will require different types of assessments. Let's look at an example to illustrate this point: the Pennsylvania Learning Standard for Early Childhood: AL.1 PK.C, *Engage in complex play sequences with two or more children.* This standard can only be assessed by watching a child engaging in play with other children. Besides the likelihood that most 3- and 4-year-olds are not able to read and write, asking students to draw or write about how to play with others, or read a story about children playing and then discuss it, is not the same as actually engaging in play themselves, as delineated in the standard. The assessment must be congruent with the standard it is intended to measure.

Now, read each of the standards in Figure 4.1 (see p. 70), and for each one place a checkmark in the column identifying the assessment that you feel can best determine student understanding. You can choose more than one type of assessment for each standard, but each assessment chosen must answer the question *Will this assessment generate reliable evidence of student learning?*

What do you notice about the relationship between the standard and the types of assessments used to determine student understanding? You may have noticed some of the points included in the following discussion.

First, many standards can be assessed by more than one type of assessment. This is particularly true of reading standards and content-specific standards. For example, RH.9-10.9, the first standard in Figure 4.1, asks students to compare and contrast how primary and secondary sources treat the same topic. An information-recall assessment might ask students to read a brief explanation of the role of Martin Luther in the Protestant Reformation and then an excerpt from his "95 Theses" and identify the statement that best explains the similarity or difference between the two passages. A product assessment could have students write an analysis of Martin Luther's role in the Reformation by comparing and contrasting primary source materials against secondary syntheses. A demonstration might have students debate his role and the role of others in the Reformation using both primary and secondary sources, and discuss the use of

Figure 4.1
CONGRUENCE IN ASSESSMENT

Standard	Type(s) of Assessment Needed			
	Recall	Product	Demon-stration	Process
RH.9–10.9 Compare and contrast treatments of the same topic in several primary and secondary sources.				
PS3.D: Energy in Chemical Processes and Everyday Life—The energy released [from] food was once energy from the sun that was captured by plants in the chemical process that forms plant matter (from air and water). (5-PS3-1)				
SL.6.5 Include multimedia components (e.g., graphics, images, music, sound) and visual displays in presentations to clarify information.				
ELD Standard 2: English language learners communicate information, ideas, and concepts necessary for academic success in the content area of Language Arts. Grade 4 Level 3—Developing: Categorize passages based on narrative points of view from illustrated text using word/phrase banks with a partner. (WIDA)				
Disposition of Practice—Commitment to Reflection: values time to think, ask questions, consider actions, evaluate activities and work, set goals, and plan future actions stemming from those goals.				

Source: © 2012 by Learner-Centered Initiatives. Used with permission.

the sources as evidence given the time, place, and conditions under which they were written.

Content-specific standards or understandings can also often be assessed in more than one way. The second example in Figure 4.1, the NGSS discipline core idea PS3.D: Energy in Chemical Processes and Everyday Life, can be assessed by information recall, product, and demonstration. An information-recall assessment would ask questions about the steps in the process; a product assessment would call for students to illustrate and explain the process; and in a demonstration, students would explain the process using a model or an illustration.

When a standard can be assessed using more than one type of assessment, it is worthwhile to do so. The use of multiple measures provides the teacher with more detailed information about what the student knows and is able to do, and under what conditions. For example, a student may have little difficulty conducting and explaining the results of a lab experiment to his classmates. However, he may have difficulty writing about it, raising questions for the teacher about whether the student's ability to articulate his understanding in writing or his level of understanding is interfering with his ability to respond.

Second, standards specific to a modality or that describe a specific action can only be assessed one way. This was true of the early childhood standard mentioned earlier and is also true of Speaking Standard 6.5, the third example in Figure 4.1. Both of these standards can only be measured using one type of assessment: demonstration. In the case of the speaking standard, students must give a presentation using multimedia tools in order for the teacher to determine if they are able to use the skills included in the standard. Although other assessments might be able to measure related understandings—for example, an information-recall assessment might provide students with a scenario about a presentation and ask them to choose the most appropriate multimedia component—it would not truly be assessing students' ability to actually give a presentation using multimedia tools.

The WIDA English Language Development (ELD) standard, the fourth example in Figure 4.1, is another one that can be assessed using one type of assessment. At first, it may seem that the best form of assessment of this standard is demonstration—a teacher observing students categorizing passages. Closer reading of the standard, however, indicates that it should be assessed using an information-recall assessment. Although students are working together, the focus of the standard is on categorizing information using a word bank, and not the process used to do so.

The last example, the dispositional standard, illustrates the need for a process assessment. The only way to discover what students are thinking is to provide them with the opportunity to share their thinking with you. You can ask students to evaluate the results of an information-recall assessment, taking note of any trends in the questions they got wrong and the reasons why they got these questions wrong, in order to set goals for improvement. They may also keep a journal documenting their decision-making process while conducting research, writing a paper, or preparing for a formal presentation. The purpose of these process assessments is to provide students with time to think, ask questions, consider actions, evaluate activities and work, set goals, and plan future actions stemming from those goals. The assessments help teachers identify needs, surface misconceptions, and make instructional decisions to support students.

Examining assessments to determine if they are congruent with the standards they intend to measure provides information about whether the curriculum includes appropriate and varied measures of student learning. Although congruence is important, there needs to be a match between what you are assessing and the way it is being assessed; congruence does not necessarily ensure strong alignment. As explained in Chapter 2, strong alignment occurs when the task and the standard are difficult to distinguish from each other and the intent of the standard remains intact. The assessments will also need to be evaluated to determine the degree of alignment to the standards.

Assessment Purposes

In addition to being aware of the types of assessments, the purpose of those assessments should be considered when examining or creating curriculum. Assessments have three purposes: diagnostic, formative, and summative. Usually these assessment purposes are associated with timing, but more important than timing is how the information is being used.

Diagnostic Assessment

Diagnostic assessment can be used to identify what students know and are able to do, to uncover misconceptions students have, and as a baseline for determining growth. It is used at the beginning of a learning cycle—meaning the beginning of a school year, a unit, a learning experience, or a lesson; and diagnostic assessment activities range in formality, depending on how the teacher plans to use the information. For example, if a 1st grade teacher wants to determine what students know about frogs, students can contribute factual information during a classroom discussion in which the teacher records their responses. This is an informal way for the teacher to determine what students know, as well as to identify any misconceptions they may have about frogs. However, if the teacher wants to also know how well her students communicate in writing, she would need to ask them to respond in writing and then examine their work to determine what they know about frogs as well as their strengths and needs as writers.

If the same 1st grade teacher wants to know about students' strengths and weaknesses as readers and then measure their growth as readers throughout the year, she would need a much more formal diagnostic demonstration assessment, such as a running record. She would use the assessment at the beginning of the year as a baseline diagnostic, at key points during the year to monitor student learning, and at the end of the year to determine growth.

Another example that illustrates the use of diagnostic assessment as a baseline at the high school level is student responses to a document-based question (DBQ). In an American history class, students might read and analyze primary and secondary sources related to colonial foundations, and then write a response to the question *What factors influenced colonial variations in economics, social hierarchy, and labor structure?* During the school year, students would engage in many learning experiences, working with primary and secondary sources, and would have other opportunities to respond to DBQs. At the end of the year, students would again use primary and secondary sources to respond to the question *What is the place of the United States today in a globalized and interconnected world?*

To determine growth, the assessment tasks must be parallel in both their skills and the conditions under which they are completed. Content may or may not be the same, depending on standards the assessment is intended to measure. The examples just described require the students to use the same skills at the beginning and end of the year, but the content changes because the focus of the assessments is on how students apply skills and not the specific content itself.

Formative Assessment

In both the 1st grade classroom and the American history classroom, the diagnostic assessment was followed by additional activities used by the teacher to monitor student understanding. These checks for understanding are formative in nature because they have been strategically planned by the teacher as opportunities for students to share their understanding with the teacher, and for the teacher to respond accordingly. The process varies in terms of the type and formality of the tasks involved, but they are all low-stakes, learning-focused activities that serve a variety of interwoven purposes:

- Check for content understanding to determine what information students have learned.
- Check for skill understanding to determine if students can apply the skills they have been taught.

- Prepare for a summative assessment through research and building background knowledge.

- Provide opportunities for teacher feedback, peer assessment, self-assessment, and revision.

- Determine next steps for instruction based on student need.

To illustrate the role of formative assessment, read the assessment description in Figure 4.2 (see p. 76). Following the directions provided, underline the formative assessment opportunities and identify the purpose. The first one has been completed for you as an example.

There are three formative assessment opportunities in the description. The first consists of writing summaries of newspaper articles, which are used to determine student understanding and decide on necessary next steps for instruction. Based on reading the student work, the teacher may choose to address the students' ability to summarize and their understanding of the content in the articles in either small groups or as a class.

The second formative assessment opportunity is the journal. Students use the journal to document their research. They meet with other students or the teacher for feedback on the accuracy of their information, and they have the opportunity to ask clarifying questions about their own work. Conferencing allows the teacher to address the individual needs of the students. It may also surface additional information about student understanding. After meeting with all the students, the teacher may notice trends in their needs and decide to address these areas in subsequent classroom lessons.

The last formative assessment opportunity is the draft of the letter. The teacher provides students with descriptive feedback addressing both the content of the information and how they communicated that information in their letter. This is the last student-teacher interaction before the letter is sent to the student's parents. The revised letter serves as the summative assessment.

Formative assessment serves a vital role in supporting and producing learning. It acts as an ongoing conversation between the teacher and the

Figure 4.2
THE ROLE OF FORMATIVE ASSESSMENT

Directions:

1. In the following description of assessment, underline the <u>formative assessment</u> opportunity—that is, the product or performance assessment that the teacher has planned to enable students to share their understanding and the teacher to respond accordingly.

2. For each assessment opportunity, choose one or more of the following purposes:

- Check for <u>content understanding</u> to determine what information students have learned.
- Check for <u>skill understanding</u> to determine if students can apply the skills they have been taught.
- Prepare for a summative assessment through research and building background knowledge.
- Provide opportunities for teacher feedback, peer assessment, self-assessment, and revision.
- Determine next steps for instruction based on student need.

The first formative assessment opportunity has been underlined in the assessment description. Its purposes are identified at the bottom of the figure.

Assessment Description

Students read several newspaper articles about the current state of the economy in the United States compared with the economies of countries in Europe and Asia. They <u>write and submit a summary</u> of each article to the teacher so she can monitor their understanding of economic conditions in different regions and provide explicit instruction in areas where students need additional information and clarification.

Students identify an item they would like to purchase. They determine the cost of the item given the current exchange rate between U.S. dollars, the euro, and a currency in Asia. Students then research the product using different websites. They determine the final price of the item on each website, including tax and shipping cost. They also determine the cost of the product including tax if it was purchased at a local store. Students <u>document their research in a journal and conference with the teacher</u> and other students to check the accuracy of their information.

Students use the information they have gathered to <u>draft a letter</u> to their parents explaining the best place to purchase the item and why. After receiving descriptive feedback on their letter from the teacher, they revise it and send it to their parents.

Purpose of the Formative Assessment Activity

Assessment Opportunity 1: Written Summary

1. Check for skill understanding—summary.
2. Check for content understanding—economics.
3. Determine next steps in instruction.

student through a feedback loop. It begins with feedback to the teacher from the students about what they have and have not learned, and continues with feedback from the teacher to the students about individual strengths and weaknesses, and what actions they can take to move forward.

As shown in the examples, formative assessment provides students with feedback in many ways: descriptive feedback from the teacher, peer conferencing, small-group discussions, rubrics, and checklists; and although all these methods of providing feedback are important, the most powerful is descriptive feedback. Descriptive feedback from the teacher provides detailed information to the students on their strengths and needs, as well as next steps for improving their work.

Summative Assessment

Summative assessment is the final assessment that provides the teacher and the students with information about what has been learned. Summative assessment tends to be high-stakes and used for evaluative and grading and reporting purposes. Although the letter in the example from Figure 4.2 may not seem like a high-stakes assessment because it is being sent to the students' parents, the letter also enables the teacher to determine what students learned about economics and their ability to communicate information. The teacher will use it for grading and reporting purposes. A quality summative assessment, such as this one, will include a rubric or checklist that communicates expectations and that the teacher will use to evaluate the written piece.

As shown in this example, a formative assessment can become a summative assessment—the draft became the final piece. The written newspaper article summaries are another opportunity for a summative assessment. The teacher could provide students with feedback to revise their summaries and submit them for a grade. The revised summaries would serve as the final assessment for that learning experience within the unit. This change in the use of assessments within the unit illustrates the importance of understanding the purpose of the assessment as the determining factor in identifying it as diagnostic, formative, or summative.

Implications for Evaluating, Creating, or Revising Curriculum

The terms used to describe assessment types and purposes have been used in education for some time. I have found that whenever education terms become prevalent, there is an assumption that all educators understand their meaning. Although this is true to a point, most likely teachers have very different understandings of these terms. Therefore, before evaluating or creating the assessments within a curriculum, it is important to establish a collective understanding of the different types of assessments and the purposes they serve. Once that has been accomplished, it is possible to evaluate the current assessments and determine which assessments to keep, eliminate, and revise.

An efficient way to evaluate assessments is to create a simple list in which you identify the type and purpose of each. Consolidating the assessments into a one-page document, as in Figure 4.3, makes analysis simple, through the use of a series of guiding questions. The first set of guiding questions focuses on the types of assessments. Here the questions have been applied to the high school global studies example in Figure 4.3.

1. *What types of assessments are used to determine student understanding?* This course uses primarily two types of assessments: information recall and product. In only one case can students choose demonstration as an option.

2. *Is there an overreliance on one type, and are any types of assessments missing?* To determine if there is an overreliance, we first need to consider why one type would be preferred over another. In this case, tests are used as an assessment in every unit. Given that this is a social studies curriculum, we can assume that teachers are using the unit test to determine what content students have learned. Although an information-recall assessment may be appropriate and is certainly very common in the classroom, in some cases this is the only type of assessment used, and students do not have any other way of sharing what they know with the teacher. In the units that include some products as

Figure 4.3

GLOBAL STUDIES ASSESSMENTS

	Assessment Description	Type*	Purpose**	Standards
Unit 1: Early Man and the Birth of Civilization	• Unit test • Essay: Where did civilization begin?	IR PD	S	9.1a–d 9.4b
Unit 2: Ancient Western Civilization	• Unit test	IR	S	9.1a, b, d 9.2a, b 9.3a 9.4b, e
Unit 3: Ancient Eastern Civilization	• Unit test • Essay: How did the Silk Road contribute to cultural diffusion?	IR PD	S	9.1c, d 9.2b 9.3b 9.4b, c
Unit 4: Middle Ages	• Unit test • Project: Students choose one of the following: 　○ Create a cause-and-effect chart showing the reasons why feudalism developed and its consequences. 　○ Role-play the various ranks in the hierarchy of feudal society and church society. 　○ Find examples of various types of art and architecture of the Middle Ages and explain how each reflects the cultural values of the time period. 　○ Read and summarize a primary source text and a secondary source text that illustrate the abusive power and corruption in society and the church during the Middle Ages. 　○ Identify and rank the reasons why people joined the Crusades.	IR PD D	S	9.4e 9.5c, d, f, g 9.6a, d

(continues)

Figure 4.3

GLOBAL STUDIES ASSESSMENTS (continued)

	Assessment Description	Type*	Purpose**	Standards
Unit 5: East Asia	• Unit test	IR	S	9.3a–c 9.4b, d 9.5a, b, d 9.6a
Unit 6: Early Modern Europe	• Unit test • DBQ: What was the impact of the European Renaissance?	IR PD	S	9.4b–d 9.6b–d
Unit 7: Age of Globalization	• Unit test • DBQ: Did the Age of Exploration change the world for the better?	IR PD	S	9.2b 9.3a 9.4d 9.5d 9.7a, c, d, f 9.8c, d

*Types: IR = Information Recall; PD = Product; D = Demonstration; PR = Process

**Purpose: D = Diagnostic; F = Formative; S = Summative

assessments, the products are in the form of essays. The only variation is the project in which students can choose from five options, including a demonstration. There are no process assessments. Based on these observations, we can conclude that the global studies course does not include a wide variety of ways to determine what students know and are able to do, and provides no opportunity for students to share their thinking processes.

3. *Are the types of assessments used congruent with the standards they intend to measure?* Social studies content standards are identified for each unit, and as stated previously, information-recall and product assessments are congruent forms for measuring content. What seem to be missing are any process types of standards, raising a question as to whether standards are missing from the curriculum or certain standards are deemed not important enough to include.

4. *Are multiple measures used when more than one type of assessment can be used to measure the same learning target?* Multiple measures are used in some units; however, the products are primarily essays, and they focus on very discrete learning within the curriculum.

With a better understanding of the types of assessments included in the curriculum, the next step is to examine the purposes they serve. The following questions can be used for this analysis:

1. *What assessment purposes are identified in the curriculum?* The curriculum lists only summative assessments.

2. *How is diagnostic assessment used?* There is no indication of diagnostic assessment.

3. *How is formative assessment used? Are there opportunities for students to receive feedback from their teachers?* No formative activities are identified.

4. *Are summative assessments designed to produce as well as measure learning?* Without the use of related diagnostic and formative assessment activities that involve feedback to the students on how they are progressing toward the standards, the summative assessments cannot be used to produce learning. The sole objective of the assessments in this curriculum is to measure what students learned.

The analysis of this curriculum reveals that it relies greatly on tests and a limited number of product assessments, all focused on measuring student learning. Assessment within a quality curriculum focuses on assessment *for* learning. This curriculum would greatly benefit from the incorporation of curriculum-embedded assessments, the focus of the next chapter.

Summary: Assessment Types and Purposes

Teachers use four types of assessments to determine what students know, are able to do, and value. These types are information recall, demonstration, product, and process assessments. A quality curriculum will include different types of assessments that are congruent with the standards for the unit. Multiple assessments are used when more than one type of assessment can be used to measure student learning, providing the teacher with multiple sources for determining what students know and are able to do.

Assessments serve three purposes; diagnostic, formative, and summative. Usually these assessment purposes are associated with timing, but more important than timing is how the information is being used. Diagnostic assessment determines what students know and are able to do, and identifies student misconceptions. It is used to determine the starting point for instruction and as a baseline for determining growth. Formative assessment serves as a check for understanding. It occurs while learning is still taking place and provides teachers with opportunities to give students descriptive feedback and to modify instruction based on student need. Summative assessment is used to determine what students have learned and is the final assessment in a learning cycle. Information recall, product, demonstration, and process assessments can all be used for these different purposes.

Tools and Activities for Evaluation, Design, and Revision

- **Congruence in Assessment Activity.** This activity (see example in Figure 4.1) is used for establishing the relationship between the different types of assessments that can be used to measure different standards. It illustrates how some standards can be measured by only one type of assessment, whereas others can and should be measured by all types of assessments.

- **Purpose of Formative Assessment Activity.** This activity (see example in Figure 4.2) is used to establish the role of formative assessment in the learning cycle. First, identify the tangible assessment—what the teacher will collect or observe—and then how the teachers will use the assessment to produce learning.

- **Assessment-Analysis Chart and Questions.** This simple chart (see example in Figure 4.3) is used to collect information about the types and purposes of the assessments that exist within the curriculum so decisions can be made as to what assessments should be kept, revised or designed, and integrated into the curriculum itself. The guiding questions in this chapter can be used to analyze the collected data.

✔ Checklist for Evaluation, Design, and Revision

☐ Multiple and varied types of assessments are used to ascertain what students know and are able to do. These assessments include information recall, product assessments, demonstrations, and process assessments.

☐ The type of assessment used to measure student learning is congruent with the standards being measured.

☐ Multiple measures are used to determine what students know and are able to do, and to identify their strengths and weaknesses as learners.

☐ The purpose of the assessment as diagnostic, formative, or summative is clearly identified and shared with the students.

☐ Diagnostic assessment identifies what students know, as well as their misconceptions. It is used as a starting point for instruction and as a baseline for measuring growth.

☐ Formative assessment is used to monitor student learning. It provides teachers with information in a way that is accessible and can be used to make instructional decisions.

☐ Formative assessment gives teachers opportunities to provide students with feedback while it still can be used. Descriptive formative assessment can greatly affect student achievement.

☐ Summative assessment is used to measure student learning.

Assessment is learning

Curriculum-Embedded Performance Assessments

Read through each of the following example sets. As you read, take note of what Assessments A and B have in common with each other and how they differ.

Example Set 1

Assessment A: Students read myths from a variety of cultures. For each myth, they complete a reader's response in which they

- Summarize the story describing the characters, plot, and setting.
- Explain how the story helped people understand the unknown.
- Compare and contrast how two myths have similar themes, topics, and patterns of events.

The teacher reads the responses to determine students' understanding of the myths. She creates small groups for instruction based on her review and identifies students to meet with during individual conferences.

Students read nonfiction texts that describe the science behind one of the stories. They summarize each text and describe what really happens and why. The teacher reads the student summaries and identifies areas where the students need additional information and clarification. She addresses these areas during subsequent science lessons.

Students write an introduction to a myth of their choice in which they

- Summarize the myth and what it was trying to explain.
- Make connections between the myth and science.
- Explain the science behind the myth.
- Use scientific language.

Students submit their introductions to the teacher for feedback. They revise the introductions and include them in a collection of myths to be housed in the school and classroom library.

Assessment B: Students read a myth and an article that both provide explanations for why mosquitos buzz. Students write an essay in which they describe how the explanations are similar and different. Students use specific examples from the myth and the article to support their answers.

In their essays, students

- Describe what the myth says about why mosquitos buzz.
- Describe what the article says about why mosquitos buzz.
- Compare and contrast the two explanations.
- Include details from both the myth and the article to support their answer.

Example Set 2

Assessment A: Students identify the different ways in which people convey their identity, and how their actions, words, and online presence make up a "personal brand." Students choose a current media figure and analyze that individual's personal brand and how it conveys this person in either a positive or a negative way.

Students analyze the state of their own personal brand, and create and implement a plan for further developing it so it reflects what they want to convey to others about their identity.

In their analysis students examine

- How they currently convey their personal brand in person, on paper, and online.

- What it conveys about them in terms of strengths, values, and passions.
- Whether their personal brand accurately reflects who they are.

In their plan, students identify changes that they can make to improve their personal brand and the steps necessary for making those changes. Students then implement and reflect on the changes they make so their personal brand better reflects who they are.

Assessment B: Students write an essay in which they discuss the power of a personal brand. In their essay, they

- Introduce and define the term *personal brand*.
- Organize their ideas and information.
- Develop their essay by including relevant facts, definitions, details, and examples.
- Use varied transitions and sentence structures to create cohesion and clarify the relationships among complex ideas and concepts.
- Use precise language and domain-specific vocabulary.
- Convey a knowledgeable stance.
- Provide a concluding statement or section that supports the information or explanation provided.

The most obvious commonality in both examples is that the content is the same in Assessments A and B. It is also apparent in both examples that students are required to use similar skills. In the first example set, students are asked to both read and write about myths. In the second example set they also write, although what they are writing about is slightly different. In Assessment A, students are writing to analyze their own personal brand and create a plan for improving upon it, whereas in Assessment B, they are writing about the impact of a personal brand. Both serve as summative assessments used to determine student understanding.

At the surface level, there doesn't appear to be much difference between the two, but the differences between them illustrate how assessments can be events whose sole purpose is to measure learning or ones that *produce assessments can produce learning*

as well as *measure* learning. Both of the A assessments take place over time and require students to make choices about their learning, resulting in a more meaningful and rigorous learning experience. The assessments include diagnostic, formative, and summative assessment activities. The students and teacher interact as the students complete different parts of the assessments. The teacher adjusts instruction based on student need, and the students receive feedback and make revisions before completing the summative assessments.

The B assessments, by contrast, are assignments or events. They are limited to a specific text, topic, or writing genre identified by the teacher with little or no student choice. These assessments serve as summative assessments with no opportunity for teacher instruction or feedback to the students. The purpose of these assessments is to measure learning.

Both assessments—A and B—have a place in the curriculum. Teachers want to know what students have independently learned as a result of instruction. However, a curriculum that relies solely on self-contained assessments is in danger of focusing exclusively on the outcome rather than the learning process itself and does little to involve the student.

A quality curriculum includes curriculum-embedded assessments that reflect the belief that assessment is learning. A curriculum in which assessment is learning is one that

- Begins as students become aware of the goals of instruction and the criteria for performance.
- Involves goal setting, monitoring progress, and reflecting on results.
- Implies student ownership and responsibility for moving thinking forward (metacognition).
- Occurs throughout the learning process. (Black & Wiliam, 1998; Wiliam, 2011)

Assessments that produce as well as measure learning are the focus of this chapter.

Features of Quality Performance Assessments

Performance assessments are those that require students to demonstrate achievement by producing an extended written or spoken answer, by engaging in group or individual activities, or by creating a specific product (Nitko, 2001; Stiggins, 1997). They are also referred to as performance-based assessments and, more recently, performance tasks.

Both of the assessments in each set introduced at the beginning of this chapter could be considered performance tasks. They both serve as summative assessments but differ in the conditions under which they are completed. The A assessments are embedded in the curriculum. The task is the final culminating piece, but the entire performance assessment takes place over time and includes diagnostic, formative, and summative assessment elements. The final performance task relies on successful implementation of the formative measures. As discussed in Chapter 4, the diagnostic measure is designed to begin the assessment process by providing the teacher with information about what the students know and their misconceptions. It can also serve as a baseline for growth when explicitly aligned with the same set of standards as the summative assessment.

The B assessments are on-demand performance tasks. They are implemented in a given time and place. Because they are separate events, they do not rely on other assessment opportunities in the same way as a curriculum-embedded performance assessment.

A quality curriculum-embedded performance task

• Measures the most important learning of the unit as articulated through the organizing center—the unit title, essential question, and big idea—which was discussed in Chapter 1.

• Includes tasks that are congruent with and strongly align to the standards. This means (1) the task includes different modalities that reflect the standards being measured, and it meets the criteria for strong alignment; (2) the task and standards are difficult to separate from each other; (3) the task requires students to fully engage in activities that align to all the skills embedded within the standard; and (4) the task honors the intent of the standards.

• Has an authentic audience and purpose. Quality performance tasks have an authentic audience and purpose that go beyond the teacher and classroom. They are designed to help students interact with the real world.

• Provides opportunity for teacher feedback and student revision. Quality performance tasks include diagnostic and formative assessment activities that provide information that the teacher can use to adjust instruction and opportunities for teachers to give students feedback that they can use to revise their work.

• Includes specific criteria for student performance. The task outlines the criteria that will be used for evaluation, and it has corresponding rubrics and checklists that can be used for instruction and feedback purposes as well as evaluation.

In the following sections, we examine each of these features in greater detail.

Measuring the Most Important Learning

In Chapter 1, I discussed in great depth the concept of quality organizing centers and how they are articulated through the unit title, the essential question, and the big idea. The purpose of the organizing center is to identify the most important learning for the unit, so it makes sense that the performance task would measure this learning. Consider the following organizing center:

Unit Title: So We All Can Eat

Essential Question: What does it take for the people of the world to feed themselves?

Big Idea: Students understand that not all people can feed themselves and that even small yet deliberate steps can be taken to end world hunger.

A performance task designed to measure this learning would include student investigations of conditions that prevent people from feeding themselves and actions that they could take to address these circumstances.

Congruence and Strong Alignment to the Standards

Congruence is the match between the standards and a task; alignment is the degree to which the task meets the standard. In Chapter 4, I explored congruence in relation to determining the type of assessment to use. An assessment designed to measure reading, writing, and listening standards would need to include those modalities. In Chapter 2, I discussed the importance of alignment throughout the curriculum and provided several activities for ensuring alignment. These activities included *Determining Alignment in a Curriculum* (see Figure 2.3) and *Coding Standards* (see example on pp. 43–44). A quality performance task must be both congruent and strongly aligned to the standards that have been identified in the unit of study.

Authentic Audience and Purpose

Although the goal of education is to prepare students for their lives after school, much of what students are asked to do is contrived and restricted to the classroom. A quality curriculum will include performance tasks that allow students to interact with the real world—that is, with real audiences and purposes.

Changing the audience and purpose greatly affects the task by making it more engaging and meaningful to the students, and by increasing the amount of thinking it requires. Let's see how this is so by returning to the example sets at the beginning of this chapter. In Example Set 1, the audience for Assessment A is the larger school community. The introductions to the myths are being included in books that will circulate to teachers and students within the school system. In Example Set 2, the real audience for Assessment A consists of the students themselves and the world that they interact with through social media. Students explore their personal brand and what it communicates as they prepare to enter college or begin jobs where others will view and use these sources to make decisions that affect the students' future.

In both cases, it is easy to see how writing for a real audience and purpose would be more engaging and meaningful to the students. Someone other than the teacher will see the work, so there is more cause to care about the completed product; it will last longer than the amount of time it takes to read or view it. The tasks also require higher levels of thinking because students need to plan, research, draft, and revise, and in doing so they use such thinking skills as synthesizing, analyzing, evaluating, and creating—all skills that fall in the upper levels of Bloom's taxonomy.

The rubric created by Learner-Centered Initiatives in Figure 5.1 (see p. 92) is a tool that you can use to evaluate the level of authenticity in performance tasks. Notice that the descriptors include not only the purpose and audience but also the degree to which students will interact with others. In most real-world situations, people do not work in complete isolation. Rather, they interact and collaborate, receiving and giving feedback to complete a task. In addition to describing the levels of authenticity, the rubric also provides an example of a science task at each level.

Opportunity for Teacher Feedback and Student Revision

A quality curriculum will ensure that the diagnostic and formative assessment opportunities are clearly identified, as shown in the following example:

Diagnostic assessment opportunity: Students create a list of questions they have about how plants grow.

Formative assessment opportunity: Students examine a variety of stories and nonfiction texts that describe how plants grow. Together the class creates an illustrated flip chart that asks and answers their questions about how plants grow.

Formative assessment opportunity: Students plant seeds and document the seeds' growth in a plant journal. Students add new information to their illustrated flip chart based on the observations of their plants.

Figure 5.1

AUTHENTICITY RUBRIC

Level 1	Level 2	Level 3	Level 4
The task is contrived and divorced from plausible or realistic problems/tasks and audiences beyond the teacher.	The task involves students in plausible problems/tasks with the class or teacher as the audience; possible audiences outside the classroom have not been identified.	The task involves students in plausible or realistic problems/ tasks with possible audiences beyond the classroom that have been identified for the students.	The task requires that students engage in real problems, operating as people do outside school, and that they demonstrate and share learning with others who can benefit; or the students find the task beneficial for themselves.
Students work independently through most, if not all, phases.	Students have opportunities to confer with others.	Students work independently at times and cooperatively at other times to research or give feedback.	Students work collaboratively and interdependently through different phases of the work to deepen each other's learning.
Example: Students respond to the essay question *How has human behavior affected the Earth's biomes?*	*Example:* Students research and present to the class information about how one of the Earth's biomes has been affected by human behavior and what they can do about it.	*Example:* Students independently write a letter, essay, or blog post in which they voice their opinion about how human behavior has affected a particular biome and suggest a course of action that would assist or benefit the biome. Students work in groups to get and give peer feedback, do research, and share evidence to support one another's claims.	*Example:* Students write a proposal in which they voice their opinion about how human behavior has affected a particular biome and suggest a course of action that would assist or benefit the biome. Students share their proposals with experts in the field and request feedback on their proposed plans. After reviewing the feedback, the class determines which plan to carry out.

Source: © 2010 by Learner-Centered Initiatives. Adapted with permission.

Performance task: Students plan and create a gardening book to give with the plant as a gift for Mother's Day. In the gardening book, students include

- A cover that identifies themselves as an author and illustrator.
- A table of contents identifying the information contained in the book.
- Information on how a seed becomes a plant.
- Information on what a plant needs to grow and how to care for this particular plant.
- Illustrations that show how a plant grows.

Clearly labeling the diagnostic and formative assessment activities assists teachers in identifying the opportunities for students to share what they are learning through a product or performance. However, simple identification does not ensure that diagnostic and formative assessment activities are used as they were intended. It is also helpful to provide guidance on how these assessment activities can be used. The chart in Figure 5.2 (see p. 94) illustrates the relationship between formative assessment activities, the opportunities students have to share what they have learned, and the way in which the teacher responds to the information.

Specific Criteria for Student Performance

Another way to ensure that the curriculum includes assessments that are used to both produce and measure learning is to check that evaluation tools such as rubrics and checklists are designed to support learning. Many of the rubrics used in the classroom are the same as or similar to those used to evaluate high-stakes assessments. The problem with using these rubrics is they were not designed as instructional tools; they were designed to be used by thousands of teachers to evaluate thousands of assessments. As a result, they are often vague and provide little concrete guidance for students.

Another concern is that there are often too many rubrics, and so students never get to internalize and personalize the criteria. A quality

Figure 5.2

FORMATIVE ASSESSMENT/FEEDBACK CYCLE

Formative Assessment Opportunities	Feedback
What opportunities has the teacher created for formative assessments?	*How does the teacher provide feedback or opportunities for peer feedback and self-reflection?*
Formative Assessment Activity 1: Students examine a variety of stories and nonfiction texts that describe how plants grow. Together the class creates an illustrated flip chart that asks and answers their questions about how plants grow.	The teacher takes note of who shares information to include on the class chart and the accuracy of the information shared to determine areas in need of clarification or further instruction.
Formative Assessment Activity 2: Students plant seeds and document the seeds' growth in a plant journal, explaining how the plant grows, what helps it to grow, and how they take care of it.	The teacher reads the student journals to determine individual students' levels of understanding.
Formative Assessment Activity 3: Students plan and draft a gardening book.

Performance Task: Students create a gardening book to give with the plant as a gift for Mother's Day. | The teacher provides individual feedback to the students as they draft their books. |

curriculum includes rubrics for the most important processes or products. For example, a science curriculum would best be supported with a scientific-inquiry or lab rubric, social studies with a document-analysis rubric, and English language arts with a literary-analysis rubric. All subjects would benefit from rubrics to guide writing and reflection.

In addition to reoccurring processes in the classroom, a curriculum benefits from task-specific rubrics for long-term, high-stakes assessments like the performance tasks described in this chapter. For example, the science proposal would benefit from a task-specific rubric that students could reference as they worked together to craft their proposal and provide their classmates with feedback. However, if a generic rubric exists, as may be the case with a narrative-writing rubric in an English language arts classroom, the teacher may choose to support it with a checklist specific to the task.

In either of these cases, what is most important is that a quality curriculum will include rubrics and checklists that are strongly aligned to the same standards that were used to design the unit of study and are included in the assessment blueprint. For example, Figure 5.3 (see pp. 96–97) is a teacher version of a rubric for 2nd graders. It is based on a unit of study designed by the 2nd grade curriculum writers team from the North Rockland School District in New York, which included Amaris Scalia and Dawn Whelan. The original standards appear in the left-hand column to ensure that the rubric descriptors reflect the expectations for the students. Carefully aligning the rubric with the standards used in the design of the assessment ensures the validity of the assessment as a means for measuring learning.

In addition to being aligned to the original standards, a rubric must meet the following criteria to have an impact on instruction:

- *Descriptors are written in terms of what is evident rather than what is missing.* Often rubrics are filled with language describing what students cannot do, and unfortunately these descriptions appear in the lower levels of the rubric, targeting students who are struggling the most. Focusing on what is missing does not provide students with the guidance they need to improve their work. Focusing on what is evident helps students to find themselves on the rubric and provides information on what they need to do to move from one level to the next. In the 2nd grade rubric in Figure 5.3, the descriptor *I end the piece with my facts* could be written as *I have no conclusion.* The statement *I end the piece with my facts* describes what is evident in the student work. The student could then read across the levels to determine what he needs to do to improve his work. The next step would be to restate his opinion. The step after that would be to write a conclusion that restates his opinion and explains what he needs to do to become healthier in the future. The purpose of the rubric then is to provide direction for student work rather than simply to judge.

Figure 5.3
WRITING RUBRIC FOR HEALTHY ME UNIT

Standards	1	2	3	4
Ideas and Content *W.2.1 Write opinion pieces in which they introduce the topic or book they are writing about, state an opinion, supply reasons that support the opinion, use linking words (e.g., because, and, also) to connect opinion and reasons, and provide a concluding statement or section.* *W.2.8 Recall information from experiences or gather information from provided sources to answer a question.*	• I begin by identifying the topic, but I do not answer the question *Am I healthy?* • I make a statement about my health. • I give a fact about health that comes from my own thinking. • The fact that I gave about health is separate from my statement about my own health. • I end the piece with my fact.	• I answer the question *Am I healthy?* by stating yes or no. • I give a reason to support my answer. • My reason comes from my own thinking and may be connected to something we did in class. • My answer and my reason are connected. • My ending is a statement of my opinion.	• I include an introduction in which I answer the question *Am I healthy?* with my opinion. • I give reasons to support my opinion. • My reasons come from my own thinking and the learning we did in class. • I use linking words (*because, also*) to make connections between my opinion and reasons. • My ending describes what I can do to stay healthy in the future.	• I introduce the topic of being healthy and then answer the question *Am I healthy?* with my opinion. • I explain the reasons I have to support my opinion. • My reasons come from my own thinking, the learning we did in class, and the readings I did in my research. • I use linking words and phrases (*because, therefore, since, for example*) to connect my opinion and reasons. • My ending describes a specific goal I have for staying healthy in the future and how I might be able to reach my goal.

Sentences and Words *L.2.1 Demonstrate command of the conventions of standard English grammar and usage when writing or speaking.* *e. Use adjectives and adverbs, and choose between them depending on what is to be modified.* *f. Produce, expand, and rearrange complete simple and compound sentences (e.g., The little boy watched the movie; The boy watched the movie; The action movie was watched by the little boy).*	• I have incomplete and complete sentences. • All of my sentences start the same way. • My words are simple.	• I have simple and complete sentences. • Most of my sentences start the same way, but I also tried a new way. • My words are simple and some are related to health.	• I have complete sentences. Some of my sentences are short and some are long. • My sentences have different beginnings. • I have some health words and describing words (adjectives and adverbs).	• I have complete sentences. Some of my sentences are short, some are long, and some are questions. • My sentences have different beginnings and are put together so my piece is easy to read. • I have health terms and describing words (adjectives and adverbs) to make my writing interesting.
Rules of Writing *L.2.2 Demonstrate command of the conventions of standard English capitalization, punctuation, and spelling when writing.*	• I use a capital letter at the beginning of every sentence and for "I." • I use some correct spelling and some inventive spelling. • I have periods at the end of my lines.	• I use a capital letter at the beginning of every sentence, for "I," and for the names of people. • My spelling is mostly correct. • I have a period at the end of every sentence.	• I use a capital letter at the beginning of every sentence, for "I," and for the names of people, places, and books. • My spelling is mostly correct, even for new words! • I correctly use endmarks (. , ! ?).	• I use a capital letter at the beginning of every sentence, for "I," for the names of people and places, and for titles of books and people. • My spelling is correct, even for the *very* hard words. • I correctly use endmarks (. , ! ?) and quotation marks.

- *Descriptors avoid subjective, value-laden, quantitative language.* Another common error in rubrics is that they are filled with subjective, value-laden language such as *some, most, consistently, good,* and *accurate.* These words, once again, do not provide students with enough information to improve their work. They are left wondering about such things as how to consistently use reasons and facts to support an opinion. In addition to value-laden language, rubrics are also filled with numbers. The descriptor in the Healthy Me rubric, *I give reasons to support my opinion,* is often found on rubrics as *I give three reasons to support my opinion.* The problem with numbers is that everyone in the class might be able to give three reasons, but those reasons would not be of the same quality; yet, according to the rubric, the students would all be demonstrating the same understanding. Numbers can often be helpful when, for example, students feel uncertain about deciding how many reasons to include; but numbers are best found on checklists or provided as a range, such as "3–5 reasons."

- *The rubric is written in language that is accessible to students and reflective of classroom practice.* A rubric that can be used as an instructional tool is written in a language that students understand. The grade level of the students and the language used in the classroom should be considered when evaluating or creating a rubric that students will reference throughout the unit as they work on completing the performance task.

Implications for Content Areas

Teachers, particularly in high school content areas with end-of-the-year state exams, are often concerned that there is no time, and therefore no place, for curriculum-embedded performance tasks. Although including a lengthy performance task in every unit may not be possible, the criteria for a quality curriculum-embedded performance task will help content-area teachers to determine where to best place such tasks. Let's look at a social studies unit with the following organizing center:

Unit Title: Movement and Interactions

Essential Question: Should the movement and interactions of people be limited or encouraged?

> **Big Idea:** Students understand that the exchange of goods and the migration of peoples have resulted in cultural diffusion with positive and negative impacts on the original culture that affect residents' reactions to new immigrants.

Cultural diffusion is an important and reoccurring theme in a global studies classroom. Many historical examples can provide students with insight into the ongoing and often controversial debate around immigration. Had the organizing center been limited to a specific event or time—for example, the examination of the Silk Road presented in Chapter 4—it would not have warranted the need for an in-depth study. Here, however, the historical significance, the possibility of diverse viewpoints, and the availability of many venues for voicing opinions support the inclusion of a task such as this one in the curriculum:

> **Performance Task:** Students explore past cultures for evidence of cultural diffusion to prepare for an in-class debate on the negative and positive impact of cultural diffusion on the original culture. Students use their understanding from this debate to analyze the current debate over immigration and its impact. They analyze articles, websites, and other media representing different points of view for legitimacy and accuracy of information presented. Students express their thoughts in relation to the current political debate using one of the venues they explored during their analysis—for example, writing a letter to a political candidate, composing a newspaper editorial, submitting a blog post, showing support for an organization.

Implications for Evaluating, Creating, or Revising Curriculum

You can use the criteria described in this chapter during the design process to ensure the creation of a high-quality, curriculum-embedded performance assessment. You can also use the criteria to evaluate and then guide the revision process for existing performance tasks. The tool in

Figure 5.4 will help you to evaluate the assessments in your curriculum and decide where to focus your efforts in their revision or where it is necessary to design new ones.

To illustrate the tool's use, let's examine a performance task from a unit that was part of the 12th grade curriculum in the North Rockland School District and was written by Nori Negron. The tool summarizes the

Figure 5.4
PERFORMANCE TASK EVALUATION TOOL

Unit Title and Assessment Description	Scale of 1–5 1 = not at all; 5 = exemplary					
	Does the task measure the most important learning of the unit?	Is the assessment congruent with and strongly aligned to the standards?	Does the assessment have an authentic audience and purpose?	Does the task incorporate diagnostic and formative assessment?	Do the assessments have rubrics and checklists that can be used for both instruction and evaluation?	Revise or Replace
Research a modern-day issue and write a story or a play in the style of the horror/gothic genre, to discuss an issue of concern in modern-day society.	3	3	1	2	1	Revise

analysis. Here is an explanation of the analysis, followed by resulting revisions based on the review of the performance task.

How well does the task measure the most important learning of the unit as articulated through the organizing center? The organizing center for the unit is the following:

> **Unit 4**: Fear Factors
>
> **Essential Question:** What are we afraid of?
>
> **Big Idea:** Students understand that literature has been used to explore universal social issues that transcend time and place, and create fear in society.
>
> **Performance Task:** Students research a modern-day issue and write a story or a play, in the style of the horror/gothic genre, to discuss an issue of concern in modern-day society.

There is a match between the performance task and the organizing center in that students will show their understanding of how literature explores societal issues by writing their own story or play exploring a current societal issue. Where the task falls short is in not necessarily addressing the concept of universal issues that transcend time and place. One way to ensure that this understanding is fully explored is to include it as a guiding question for reading, research, or discussion—for example, *In what ways has this issue existed during different times and in different societies?*

Is the assessment congruent with and strongly aligned to the standards? The following standards were identified as those that would be taught and assessed in this unit of study:

> CCLS: English Language Arts 6–12, Grades 11–12, Reading: Literature
>
> RL.12.1   Cite strong and thorough textual evidence to support analysis of what the text says explicitly as well as inferences drawn from the text, including determining where the text leaves matters uncertain.

RL.12.2   Determine two or more themes or central ideas of a text and analyze their development over the course of the text, including how they interact and build on one another to produce a complex account; provide an objective summary of the text.

RL.12.3   Analyze the impact of the author's choices regarding how to develop and relate elements of a story or drama (e.g., where a story is set, how the action is ordered, how the characters are introduced and developed).

RL.12.6   Analyze a case in which grasping a point of view requires distinguishing what is directly stated in a text from what is really meant (e.g., satire, sarcasm, irony, or understatement).

CCLS: English Language Arts 6–12, Grades 11–12, Writing

W.12.3   Write narratives to develop real or imagined experiences or events using effective technique, well-chosen details, and well-structured event sequences.

   a. Engage and orient the reader by setting out a problem, situation, or observation and its significance, establishing one or multiple point(s) of view, and introducing a narrator and/or characters; create a smooth progression of experiences or events.

   b. Use narrative techniques, such as dialogue, pacing, description, reflection, and multiple plot lines, to develop experiences, events, and/or characters.

   c. Use a variety of techniques to sequence events so that they build on one another to create a coherent whole and build toward a particular tone and outcome (e.g., a sense of mystery, suspense, growth, or resolution).

   d. Use precise words and phrases, telling details, and sensory language to convey a vivid picture of the experiences, events, setting, and/or characters.

   e. Provide a conclusion that follows from and reflects on what is experienced, observed, or resolved over the course of the narrative.

First, let's examine these standards in terms of congruence with the task. The standards represent the modalities of reading and writing. The task requires students to write, and although writing can be used to assess reading, the writing task does not require students to specifically respond to what they have read. To be congruent, the task would need to include specific information about what students were reading, why, and how they would share their understanding of the text. The following revision addresses congruence with the reading standards:

> *Revision 1:* Students read and respond to a novel, novel excerpts, short stories, and movies that illustrate the use of the horror or gothic genre to explore social issues in different times and places. Students research a modern-day issue and write a story or play in the style of the horror/gothic genre to discuss an issue of concern in modern-day society.

The task and standards also lack congruence in that there are no standards to guide the research component of the task. Additional standards will need to be added for this purpose. A possible standard that could support research is W.12.7: *Conduct short as well as more sustained research projects to answer a question (including a self-generated question) or solve a problem; narrow or broaden the inquiry when appropriate; synthesize multiple sources on the subject, demonstrating understanding of the subject under investigation.*

Once the task is congruent with the standards, it is time to determine how well it aligns to the identified standards. As suggested in Chapter 2, one way to determine alignment is to code the standards into the task. Because the purpose of this review is to identify areas in need of revision, the term *potentially* has been included in the coding process to indicate where revision would be needed in order to strongly align to a standard.

> Students read and respond to a novel, novel excerpts, short stories, and movies that illustrate the use of the horror or gothic genre to explore social issues in different times and places (potentially RL.12.1, RL.12.2, RL.12.3, RL.12.6). Students research

a modern-day issue (potentially W.12.7) and write a story or play in the style of the horror/gothic genre to discuss an issue of concern in modern-day society (W.12.3).

As you can see, although alignment is evident, it certainly would not be considered strong alignment. The description of the task as written might be sufficient as an overview but does not include the detail necessary for ensuring strong alignment; too much is simply left to chance. Although the skills embedded in the standards may occur, they also may not. Here is one way to revise the task for stronger alignment:

> *Revision 2:* Students read and respond to a novel, novel excerpts, short stories, and movies that illustrate the use of the horror or gothic genre to explore social issues in different times and places. For each, they
>
> - Provide a summary of the text (RL.12.2).
> - Identify and examine how the text reflects the society of the time and place in which it is set; identify and examine the social issue explored in the text; analyze how the social issue is developed over the text and reflects the fears of the society given the time and place in which it was written (RL.12.2).
> - Analyze the author's choices regarding the development and relationship of story elements in conveying the relevance of the social issue given the time and place in which it was written (RL.12.3).
> - Analyze how the author uses satire, sarcasm, irony, understatement, or other literary technique to convey his point of view regarding the social issue (RL.2.6).
>
> Students research a modern-day social issue using a variety of sources (W.12.7) in order to plan and write a story or play (W.12.3) in the style of the horror/gothic genre. In their story or play, students
>
> - Set out the issue of concern and its significance (W.12.3a).
> - Establish one or multiple point(s) of view (W.12.3a).

- Introduce a narrator and/or characters (W.12.3a).

- Use narrative techniques to develop experiences, events, and/or characters illustrating the issue and its impact (W.12.3b).

- Use a variety of techniques to sequence and create a smooth progression of events and build toward a particular outcome (W.12.3a, W.12.3c).

- Use precise words and phrases, telling details, and sensory language to convey a vivid picture of the experiences, events, setting, and/or characters (W.12.3d).

- Provide a conclusion that reflects on what is experienced, observed, or resolved over the course of the narrative (W.12.3e).

With the task fully described and the standards coded into the task, it is much easier to see and ensure alignment. In addition, the criteria that will be used for evaluation have been built into the assessment and can easily be developed into a checklist or rubric.

The full description also serves as an assessment blueprint. Most educators are familiar with test blueprints, but developing assessment blueprints has not received the same emphasis. The assessment blueprint illustrates the relationship between the performance task and the standards. By demonstrating alignment, the assessment blueprint supports the performance task as a valid and legitimate means for determining what students know and are able to do.

Does the assessment have an authentic audience and purpose? Using the rubric to assess the level of authenticity of the task in Figure 5.4, we find that even with the revisions made so far, it can only be categorized as a Level 2 for this criterion. Asking students to write a story or play in the style of the horror/gothic genre is plausible in that there are people who do so in the real world; but as written, the description of the performance task has not identified the potential audience, and the task is confined to the classroom. By answering the question *Who would want to read these*

assessment blueprint

stories? the task could be set in a real-world situation. Consider the following possibility:

> With the success of *The Walking Dead,* AMC is considering proposals for a new series in the horror/gothic genre. Write a treatment or spec that you would propose as the basis for the new show. Include a pitch in which you explain how your treatment or spec reflects the key elements of horror/gothic classics and a social issue of the past or our society today.

This example reflects a task that is plausible but not necessarily real, because AMC may or may not choose to read student submissions. A real audience who would benefit from the students' work is the high school drama club, whose members might be willing to choose and perform one of the plays, or a print or online literary magazine that specializes in the publication of young adult work. By setting the task in a real context, such as submitting student specs and treatment to AMC, the task moves to a Level 3. By changing the audience to one that is actually real and would benefit from the work, such as the drama club, the task moves to a Level 4 on the rubric.

How does the task incorporate diagnostic and formative assessment? Now if we return to the last revision made to the high school task, we can see that the formative assessment opportunities have already been built into the task. Clarity in terms of the use of the formative assessment activities and the integration of a diagnostic will lead to the final revision:

Revision 3

Diagnostic: Students participate in a class discussion about the different social issues facing society, whether these issues existed in the past, and how literature both current and classical has reflected these issues. Students then write an individual response to these questions.

Formative Assessment Activity 1: Students read and respond to a novel, novel excerpts, short stories, and movies that illustrate the use of the horror or gothic genre to explore social issues in different times and places. For each, they

- Provide a summary of the text (RL.12.2).

- Identify and examine how the text reflects the society of the time and place in which it is set; identify and examine the social issue explored in the text; analyze how the social issue is developed over the text and reflects the fears of the society given the time and place in which it was written (RL.12.2).

- Analyze the author's choices regarding the development and relationship of story elements in conveying the relevance of the social issue given the time and place in which it was written (RL.12.3).

- Analyze how the author uses satire, sarcasm, irony, under-statement, or other literary technique to convey his or her point of view regarding the social issue (RL.12.6).

The teacher uses this information to monitor student understanding and adjusts instruction and conferences with students in small groups or independently based on their understanding of the texts.

Formative Assessment Activity 2: Students research a modern-day social issue using a variety of sources (W.12.7). They meet in small groups to share information and clarify any misunderstandings. The teacher reads the students' research and provides them with questions for clarification and elaboration.

Formative Assessment Activity 3: Students plan and draft a treatment or spec (W.12.3) that they would propose for performance by the school drama club or inclusion in the school's literary magazine.

Formative Assessment Activity 4: Students write a pitch letter in which they explain how their story/play reflects the key elements of horror/gothic classics and a social issue of the past or present. Students work in small groups to receive feedback on their pitch letters.

Performance Task: Students submit the final version of their treatment or spec (W.12.3) along with their pitch letter, in which they

- Set out the issue of concern and its significance (W.12.3a).
- Establish one or multiple point(s) of view (W.12.3a).
- Introduce a narrator and/or characters (W.12.3a).
- Use narrative techniques to develop experiences, events, and/or characters illustrating the issue and its impact (W.12.3b).
- Use a variety of techniques to sequence and create a smooth progression of events and build toward a particular outcome (W.12.3a, W.12.3c).
- Use precise words and phrases, telling details, and sensory language to convey a vivid picture of the experiences, events, setting, and/or characters (W.12.3d).
- Provide a conclusion that reflects on what is experienced, observed, or resolved over the course of the narrative (W.12.3e).

Clearly identifying the different assessment activities and how they can be used changes the assessment from one whose sole purpose is to measure learning to one that is used to both produce and measure learning. Learning takes place through the interactions of the students and the teacher. The students inform the teacher of their level of understanding through key moments in the learning process, and the teacher is able to respond to their needs, changing instruction and providing them with feedback.

Do the assessments have rubrics and checklists that can be used for both instruction and evaluation? To guide instruction and reliably assess the finished product, a rubric would need to be developed following the guidelines presented earlier in this chapter. The first steps have already been taken, because the criteria have already been laid out in the assessment description.

Once curriculum-embedded assessments are in place within the curriculum, it is possible to take a look at quality instruction that will be needed to support them. This topic is the focus of Chapter 6.

Summary: Curriculum-Embedded Performance Assessments

Assessments can be used to produce as well as measure learning if they are embedded in the curriculum and not events separate from the classroom.

Quality performance tasks measure the most important learning for the unit as articulated through the organizing center. They are congruent and strongly aligned to the standards identified in the unit and included in the performance assessment blueprint. They have an authentic audience and purpose. Performance tasks include diagnostic and formative assessment activities that provide teachers with information to adjust instruction to meet student needs, and provide students with opportunities to receive descriptive feedback from their teachers. Performance tasks include rubrics and checklists that can be used as instructional as well as evaluative tools.

Tools and Activities for Evaluation, Design, and Revision

- **Performance Task Criteria**—You can use the five criteria for performance tasks included in this chapter to either evaluate or design new tasks that produce as well as measure learning.

- **Authenticity Rubric** (Figure 5.1)—This rubric can help you to determine the level of authenticity of a performance task, and it can provide guidance on how to increase the authenticity.

- **Performance Task Evaluation Tool** (Figure 5.4)—This easy-to-use chart for evaluating the assessments in the curriculum uses a scale of 1 through 5 to answer questions related to the criteria for performance tasks. Based on your answers, you can decide which performance tasks need to be revised or replaced.

Checklist for Evaluation, Design, and Revision

A quality curriculum includes performance tasks that

- ☐ Produce as well as measure learning.
- ☐ Are embedded in the curriculum.
- ☐ Measure the most important learning as articulated in the organizing center.
- ☐ Are congruent and strongly aligned to the standards used in the design of the unit and included in the performance task assessment blueprint.
- ☐ Are connected to diagnostic and formative measures.
- ☐ Include rubrics and checklists that can be used for instructional and evaluative purposes.

Instruction

Imagine walking down a school hallway and visiting several classrooms. Here is what you see:

In the first classroom, the students sit at their desks in the dim light. The teacher stands in front of the classroom with an image of the preamble to the Constitution projected on the screen behind her. She reads it aloud to the students and stops periodically to ask them to share definitions of the words in the preamble. As they do, she paraphrases their definitions to create a new version of the preamble. At the end of class, students copy the revised version into their notebooks. The next day students learn about the articles of the Constitution.

In the next classroom, students are working in small groups. Each group has a copy of the preamble to the Constitution and has been assigned one of the words in the preamble. The students have access to a variety of texts and online resources. They use these resources to define and illustrate the word they have been given. In addition, the students create a sentence and find an antonym and a synonym for the word. As the students are working, the teacher is circulating among them, stopping to answer questions. At the end of class, the students create a classroom word wall that they will reference as they further explore these words and find examples of what the terms mean in the United States today.

In the last classroom, small groups of students are working with definitions of the words in the preamble to the Constitution. Each group is creating a chart in which they provide an example and a nonexample of the words. The teacher visits each group as they work to provide students with feedback. At the end of class, the groups post and view the charts. As they view the charts, they use checkmarks to indicate agreement or understanding of the example or nonexample, and a question mark to indicate disagreement or confusion. After class, the teacher will view student responses to determine which words need further exploration and examples before proceeding with a study of how the meanings of these words have changed over time, and their meaning in today's society.

In which classroom would you like to be a student? Most likely you would prefer the second or third classroom, where students are up and about, and engaged in very purposeful learning. These classrooms embody principles of teaching for understanding: students are engaged in meaning making with the goal of applying their knowledge to their lives, and the teacher is serving as the facilitator of this learning (McTighe & Seif, 2014). These classrooms also incorporate aspects of quality instruction for social studies, in which students engage in disciplined inquiry to construct knowledge of facts, vocabulary, concepts, and theories specific to the domain and use them to develop and express an in-depth understanding (Scheurman & Newmann, 1998). These classrooms blend these principles with an understanding of best practices in vocabulary instruction. Students are engaging with high-quality words with the intent of internalizing them so they become part of the students' expressive vocabulary (Beck, McKeown, & Kucan, 2002).

How did these teachers decide on their lessons for the day? Although it is evident that they were all teaching lessons related to the preamble, why weren't they teaching the same way? Why was the first teacher's classroom so different from the third teacher's classroom? These are all good questions, and in this chapter we answer them by focusing on how a quality curriculum addresses instruction. First, we examine what information teachers need in order to make informed decisions about classroom instruction, and then we look at the types of lessons that should be included in a curriculum.

Addressing Daily Instruction

When I work with teachers to design or revise curriculum, they often want to start by describing their lessons. This is understandable, given that their primary responsibility is to work with students on a daily basis, which means having something for the students to do. It may take some time, but the teachers eventually realize the value of having standards identified and assessments in place before describing instruction.

Not knowing the outcome first would be like driving a car without a specific destination—you would start off in one direction and make stops along the way, but eventually you would be forced to end somewhere, whether intentionally or not. Although this might work for some, most people have only a limited amount of time and resources, making such a trip unreasonable. In schools, the biggest commodity is time. There just isn't enough time for this random approach to work, so making sure the standards and assessments are in place, as described so far in this book, is the first step in generating quality learning experiences. Teachers know where their students need to be, and that knowledge sets the context and rationale for the lessons they will use in their classrooms.

A quality curriculum contains information for daily lessons that describes what students will do, why they will do it, and what evidence the teacher will have of student learning. To illustrate this, read the examples in Figure 6.1 (see p. 114) and for each identify *what* the students will do, *why*, and *how* the teacher will know, in the appropriate column. You may not be able to answer all questions for each example.

All of the tasks in Figure 6.1 were designed with the same standard in mind—RST. 6-8.1: *Cite specific textual evidence to support analysis of science and technical texts.* They differ in that each description communicates the same task with varying degrees of information and varying degrees of alignment, as discussed in Chapter 2.

The first description is a simple restatement of what students need to be able to do: identify the details in the text. It does not provide the teacher with information about how the students will do this and what evidence

Figure 6.1

IDENTIFYING WHAT, WHY, AND HOW

Description	What?	Why?	How?
Example 1: Students identify important details in the article "Disruptions: Minecraft, an Obsession and an Educational Tool," by Nick Bilton.			
Example 2 Minilesson: • The teacher identifies the learning target for the day: identifying important information that supports a claim. • The teacher introduces the article "Disruptions: Minecraft, an Obsession and an Educational Tool," by Nick Bilton, and writes a sentence that she feels best describes the point the author is trying to make. • The teacher reads the first paragraph of the article aloud to the class. • She uses a T-chart on the interactive whiteboard to write down the important details, explanations or descriptions, and her thinking as to why the information is important. • After writing down the important information, the teacher decides if the detail, explanation, or description supports her original claim. If it does, she places a checkmark next to it. If it does not, she either revises her original thinking or puts an X next to the information on the T-chart. • Several students add to the teacher's T-chart, using information from the next paragraph of the article. • The teacher reminds the students of their learning target before they begin work. Practice: Students read and complete a T-chart using the remainder of the article with a partner. As the students work, the teacher answers student questions and monitors their progress. Share: At the end of class, the students share one detail with the class, and the teacher records the details on the interactive whiteboard. The teacher collects the T-charts from the students to determine how well they were able to identify key details, and the next steps for instruction.			
Example 3 Students • Read the article "Disruptions: Minecraft, an Obsession and an Educational Tool," by Nick Bilton, and write a statement that identifies the author's claim. • Use a T-chart to record important details and explain why those details are important. • Use a checkmark to confirm which details in their chart are important in supporting the author's claim.			

there will be of student learning. As a result, there is no alignment to the standard because there is no embedded task.

By contrast, the second example is very descriptive. It identifies what the students will do—create a T-chart identifying important information; why they will do it—in order to identify important information from a text that can be used to support a claim; and what the teacher will have as evidence of student learning—T-charts. In addition, it explains what the teacher will do: read, model, demonstrate, provide feedback, and collect student work. This description can be considered a lesson plan because it contains information about both teacher and student actions. The lesson moderately aligns to the standard because although the students deeply engage with the process of identifying important details that support the author's claim, the claim (analysis) was identified by the teacher.

The last example is a series of learning experiences. They serve as the basis of lessons but are not lessons themselves because they do not describe teacher actions but instead focus on the student. Each learning experience describes what the students will do: read and write a statement identifying the author's claim, record important details from the text and explain their importance, and use a checkmark to confirm the details that support the claim. There is also information about why the students engage in these activities: identify an author's claim and distinguish important from unimportant details that support an author's claim. Each learning experience includes evidence of learning: the statement and the T-chart. Individually the learning experiences only moderately align to the standard because they focus on discrete skills. Collectively, however, the learning experiences are strongly aligned.

Each of these approaches to communicating instruction has advantages and disadvantages. Some teachers may feel that the learning target, as shown in Example 1, is all they need to design a classroom lesson. But in a curriculum, these vague statements leave too much open to interpretation, and for teachers new to a grade level or new to teaching, they simply do not offer enough support. These short statements are more appropriate for a section of the curriculum labeled "teaching points" or "learning targets."

Descriptive lessons such as the one in Example 2 can serve a purpose within a curriculum because they provide specific directions as to what should happen during the lesson, give structure to individual tasks, and illustrate the relationship between the teacher and student as part of the learning process. However, these types of lessons can also be prescriptive and cumbersome, including so much detail that they provide actual scripts of what the teacher and students will say. Sometimes teachers and administrators alike interpret lessons as nonnegotiable, meaning they must be implemented as written in the sequence set by the curriculum document—a practice that contradicts differentiated instruction, which is built on the premise that content, products, or processes can be purposefully adjusted to meet students' needs, interests, and learning styles (Tomlinson, 2014). Fully scripted lessons can also result in a lengthy and unwieldy document if the curriculum is printed on paper, making it difficult for teachers to find the most pertinent information and, ultimately, less likely that it will be used.

There is, of course, a place for such lessons, particularly if they are developed by the teachers using the curriculum. If designed to include instructional practices that support student understanding and reflect school and classroom values, these in-depth lessons can serve as excellent models for how to implement curriculum in a meaningful way. If the curriculum is housed electronically (a topic discussed in Chapter 8), links can be created from the primary curriculum document to these detailed lessons, or a separate resource document can be created to accompany a paper document.

The learning experiences in Example 3 focus on student actions. By doing so, they support the intent of standards as *learning* standards rather than *teaching* standards because they avoid emphasizing the teacher as the center of learning. Each learning experience includes information about why the student is completing the task, thus identifying the learning goal along with the activity. Including the goal in the learning experience allows the teacher to see the connection between what the students are going to learn and what they are going to do. A learning target theory of action calls for teachers to design the right target for the day's lesson and to use it along with their students to aim for and assess student understanding (Brookhart & Moss, 2014). Embedding learning targets in the learning experience makes the sharing of these goals with students much easier. Learning experiences also include evidence of student learning—what the teacher will observe or collect. This evidence serves as part of the formative assessment process to monitor student understanding, allowing the teacher to adjust instruction based on students' needs, as discussed in Chapter 4.

The benefit of addressing instruction through a series of learning experiences is that besides being clear and concise, they allow teacher flexibility in that they can be used in many different ways. For example, in primary grades, a learning experience such as "Students use the page borders of Jan Brett's *Hedgie's Surprise* to ask questions about what will happen next in the story" can be completed during a large-group discussion, in student partnerships at a learning center, or independently in a notebook. The teacher can also determine how to best support the students. The teacher may choose to model how to ask and answer questions before students begin their work, or she may choose to work with small groups of students on specific strategies for helping them to ask questions.

The caution here is that learning experiences address learning goals, which are often not standards but rather subsets of standards. As a result, by themselves they do not always strongly align to the standards and need to be used in conjunction with each other for strong alignment to occur. They may need to be grouped, as in Example 3, to show a complete task that aligns to the standards.

Another caution is that learning experiences do not provide a structure for instruction. They could be interpreted literally, which might eliminate instructional practices that support learning, such as teacher modeling or students working with a partner or in a small group. To address this, teachers will need opportunities through professional learning communities and professional development to examine instructional practices and use learning experiences to codevelop and share lessons, differentiate instruction, and sequence learning experiences (a topic discussed in Chapter 8).

Both lessons and learning experiences have their advantages and disadvantages. When evaluating curriculum or determining how to best address instruction within your curriculum, it is important to ensure that either the lesson or the learning experience clearly describes what students will do, why they will do it, and the evidence the teacher has of student learning; and to determine how strongly the lessons or learning experiences align to the standards of the unit.

Types of Learning Experiences

The types of learning experiences included in a curriculum are driven by the types of standards in the unit. In the introduction to this book, I discussed three types of standards: content, process, and disposition. Given the different types of standards, a curriculum needs different types of learning experiences, generally categorized under similar terms.

Content Learning Experiences

Content learning experiences focus on the *what*. They primarily align to discipline-specific standards, focusing on content or conceptual understandings. For example, the following is a content standard and related performance indicator from the American Psychological Association's *National Standards for High School Psychology Curricula*:

> Biological Bases of Behavior Content Standard 1: Structure and function of the nervous system in human and non-human animals
>
> 1.2   Students are able to identify the parts of the neuron and describe the basic process of neural transmission.

The standard and the performance indicator clearly identify what the student needs to know but not how the student will learn the parts of the neuron and how they work. The learning experience provides ideas on how this might be accomplished, as shown in the following example:

Students

- Create and label a model of a neuron from materials such as clay, Styrofoam, beads, and pipe cleaners, using a different color to represent each part.

- Use their models to demonstrate and explain how neurons communicate with each other.

Both of these learning experiences communicate what the students will do—create a model and use the models to illustrate how neurons communicate; why the students will complete these activities—to identify the parts of the neuron and how they work; and the evidence the teacher will have of student learning—the models and the demonstration. The learning experiences are thus designed around principles for teaching for understanding—the students are constructing their own learning. Without examples of learning experiences, standards such as the one referenced here could easily lead to a teacher-centered lesson with the teacher using a diagram to point out the parts of a neuron and explaining how they work while the students sit passively watching or copying the information into a notebook.

Process Learning Experiences

Process learning experiences focus on the *how*. They align to process standards that describe how the students will engage with the content (for example, by synthesizing, analyzing, comprehending); follow steps in a procedure such as a lab experiment or a design protocol; or communicate what they have learned (for example, through speaking or writing). The following are two examples of how learning experiences focus on process.

The first example comes from Thomas C. Giordano Middle School 45 in the Bronx in New York City. A group of teachers—Dalainy Amador,

Christina Capuano, Kiera Fox, Shawn Rawlins, and Ramonita Torres—worked with school principal Annamaria Giordano Perrotta and the administrative team—Steven Bennett, Celestine Calpin, Joan Ingram, and Filomena Mannan—to explore student discourse, participation, and engagement. Their efforts led them to design the rubric shown in Figure 6.2 (see pp. 121–123), which aligns with speaking and listening standards, and research on discourse, participation, and engagement.

The goal was to design a tool that students could use to guide their engagement in academic discourse. Once the tool was designed, however, the group discussed the fact that its success would depend on student understanding of the rubric itself, and so the first step would be to teach the students the expectations contained in the rubric. Here is the first set of learning experiences developed by this team:

Students

- **Read the <u>rubric</u> and use the following <u>text marks to code</u> their** *understanding of the rubric.*

    + This makes sense to me; I know what to do.

    ? I have a specific question about this.

    - This is not clear; I'm not sure what this means.

- **<u>Discuss</u> the following questions to** *establish student understanding of the vocabulary and information* **contained in the rubric:**

    – What parts of the rubric made sense to you? What parts clearly explain what you need to do to participate and engage in discourse in the classroom?

    – What specific questions do you have about the rubric?

    – What parts are unclear?

- **View a video of students working together and use <u>the rubric</u> to assess** the group's *ability to engage in discourse.*

- **<u>Role-play</u> different levels of expectations** found on the rubric to *clarify language and meaning.*

- **Participate in a <u>group discussion</u> to** *apply the expectations found at Level 3,* **and self-assess their efforts by completing the <u>rubric</u>.**

Figure 6.2

RUBRIC FOR DISCOURSE, PARTICIPATION, AND ENGAGEMENT (DPE)

Discourse:	1	2	3	4
• Content—addresses the topic or question	• The question is not the focus of my conversation.	• I focus on the question at the beginning of the discussion or when directed to but would rather talk about other topics.	• I address the question during the discussion; I may ask questions to clarify information.	• I address the question during the discussion; I add my own questions to guide the discussion or clarify the information.
• Evidence—uses text, details, references to support claims and ideas	• If I share anything, it is based solely on my opinion.	• I use a combination of subject-specific evidence and personal opinion during the discussion.	• I use subject-specific evidence such as text, details, and examples during the discussion.	• I use subject-specific evidence such as text, details, examples, and background knowledge during the discussion.
• Language—uses subject-specific language	• I use everyday language or slang and do not include subject-specific vocabulary.	• I use subject-specific, common vocabulary that has been emphasized in my classroom to explain my ideas, or I try to use vocabulary but use it incorrectly.	• I use subject-specific vocabulary to explain and clarify my ideas.	• I use precise, subject-specific vocabulary as well as sophisticated language to clarify my ideas.
• Dialogue—builds off the comments and questions of others; the back and forth of conversation	• I say little or nothing at all.	• I think about what I want to say but do not always actively listen to what others say; I mimic or say the same thing as others in my group.	• I add to the information and ideas shared by others by using accountable talk stems as well as my own transitions and connections.	• I make specific connections and additions to the information and ideas shared by others using language that extends accountable talk stems.

(continues)

Figure 6.2

RUBRIC FOR DISCOURSE, PARTICIPATION, AND ENGAGEMENT (DPE) (continued)

Participation:	1	2	3	4
• Process—follows a protocol or structure (examples: Socratic seminar, fishbowl, talking chips, conversation maps, tossing the ball)	• I find it difficult to follow the protocol. I may not follow directions, I won't always share my thoughts and opinions, or I may refuse to carry out my role and sit and do nothing.	• I start off following the steps of the protocol or structure but lose focus and fade until my teacher redirects me, or I make up my own rules for participating in the protocol or structure.	• I follow the steps of a protocol or structure to participate in the discussion. I may ask questions when I need clarification.	• I follow the protocol or structure and demonstrate leadership by asking others questions and encouraging everyone to fulfill their roles.
• Responsibility—manages behavior; demonstrates self-awareness; is respectful to others; follows directions	• I behave in a way that disrupts the discussion by being off task or disrespectful to others, or I don't participate at all.	• I can participate in the discussion. I may on occasion alternate between being on and off task, dominate the discussion, or shy away, but I am able to self-correct or listen to a redirection and in the end complete the task.	• I demonstrate that I am responsible for my behavior by participating in the discussion. I stay on task, cooperate with my partner or group, and am respectful of others' ideas and feelings.	• I am responsible for my own behavior in the discussion by using appropriate eye contact, adequate volume, and clear pronunciation. I redirect my group members and/or maintain the focus of the group. I am respectful and considerate of others' ideas and feelings.

Engagement:			
• Demonstrates active interest, concern, or feeling	• I don't care what others think and how my lack of interest will affect them; I don't do what needs to be accomplished. • It is easy for others to figure out that I am disinterested as seen through my body language and actions.	• I drift in and out of the discussion, participating in the parts that I find interesting, or I do what has to get done. • I complete the task or have a conversation only when it's necessary, even though it is easy to see I am not really interested in the content.	• I am present and focused, as seen through my body language and eye contact. I am involved in what I am doing by saying, showing, and working with others. • I find value in the conversation and in what others share, and I am open to new thoughts and ideas.	• I am motivated to share; I listen to and provide feedback in my interactions with the other members of the group. • I understand and appreciate the value and learning that results from sharing and working with others.

Source: From MS 45 Discourse, Participation, and Engagement Rubric and Lesson by Dalainy Amador, Christina Capuano, Kiera Fox, Shawn Rawlins, Ramonita Torres, Annamaria Giordano Perrotta, Steven Bennett, Celestine Calpin, Joan Ingram, and Filomena Mannan. Used with permission.

As you can see through the coding (boldface, italics, and underlining), each learning experience identifies **what the students will do,** *why the students will do it,* and the evidence of learning. What is missing from the learning experiences is the content. The content would depend on which class conducts the introductory lessons. The focus, however, remains the same: how do you engage in academic discourse?

The second example combines process with content. Elementary students are introduced to electrical and magnetic forces by participating in learning experiences aligned to the ISTE standard for Research and Information Fluency: students apply digital tools to gather, evaluate, and use information.

Students

- **Use a search tool** (key word, sidebar, hyperlink) *to locate information* on electrical or magnetic interactions. They share the strategy with a student who used a different search tool for research.

- **Use a bookmarking program** to *identify* 3–5 *resources that could possibly contain useful information and digital tools* explaining how magnetic or electrical interactions work.

- Revisit their resources and **use a highlighting tool** *to identify important information that answers who, what, where, why, and when questions* about either electrical or magnetic interactions. Students eliminate any of the resources that are not helpful in answering the questions.

- **Summarize** the *information they have learned* by sharing it with a partner. They create a written summary after participating in the peer sharing session.

The primary focus of this series of learning experiences is on learning how to use research tools. The secondary focus is on the information itself. As students use the research tools, they are also developing background knowledge on electrical and magnetic interactions that will come in handy as they proceed with the unit. After learning how to use these research tools, student will participate in other learning experiences that focus on the design of an experiment for testing their understanding of how either electrical or magnetic forces work. During the next series of learning experiences, the primary and secondary focuses will change. The primary focus will be on developing student understanding of how electrical and magnetic interactions occur, with students using their research skills to support their learning.

Dispositional Learning Experiences

Dispositional or metacognitive learning experiences focus on student thinking. The term *metacognition* simply means "thinking about thinking." Just as students need to be taught content and skills, students also need time to develop their ability to reflect and think about their thinking. Let's examine this idea by looking at the following example of a series of learning experiences that address metacognition.

Students

- **Examine samples of student reflections** in response to the following prompts and **use sticky notes to tag** those that *best explained what the student was thinking.*

  - What did you learn that was new today?
  - What helped you to learn today?
  - What did you struggle with?
  - What are some things you can do or the teacher can do to help you in the areas you struggled with?

- **Reread the student samples that were tagged and write on the sticky note** *what made it easy to read and understand what the student was thinking.*

- **Contribute criteria to a class checklist** *identifying characteristics of quality reflection.*

- **Answer the same questions** after participating in a series of lessons, and **self-assess their reflection** using the class checklist. Students *improve their reflection* by **revising it** based on their self-assessment.

The focus of these learning experiences is on the quality of the thinking and not on what the students are thinking about, although the answers to these reflective prompts will provide teachers with great insight into student understanding and misconceptions. Previous learning experiences may have focused on establishing the rationale for metacognition, and future learning experiences can assist students in using their ability to reflect as they set and monitor goals—all of which can contribute to improving learning. Also notice that the learning experiences are not grade-specific. All students, regardless of their age, can be taught to share and reflect on their thinking. The degree and sophistication of their thinking and the language used to describe it might change, but the ability to reflect exists and can be tapped at any age.

The following example illustrates the connection between metacognition and process by integrating the two into the same series of learning experiences. In this example, students are writing a marketing proposal for the school's yearly fundraiser.

Students

- *Are introduced to a warm and cool feedback protocol* by **reading examples of both** in response to a draft proposal written by a former student. After reading the proposal and feedback, they **check off those points that they agree with.**

- Read a draft proposal written by another student and **write down their own warm and cool feedback. Students compare their feedback points with those of a partner** to *determine how their feedback could affect the writing.*

- **Watch a small group give feedback to one of its members using the warm and cool feedback strategy, and <u>discuss</u> the** *quality of the feedback and how it could affect the proposal.*

- **<u>Participate</u> in small-group warm and cool feedback** using their own piece of writing so they can *further revise and edit their own proposals.*

Peer Review Process for Warm and Cool Feedback

(Note: The following steps outline how to conduct peer review for warm and cool feedback, a process originally developed by Blythe, Allen, and Powell [1999].)

1. Each presenter shares his or her work for 3–5 minutes while members of the group listen and take notes.
2. Each member of the group shares one piece of warm feedback.
3. The same procedure is followed for cool feedback.
4. The presenter can take notes while the sharing is occurring but cannot respond to questions or comments.
5. The group should go through at least one full round of warm feedback before shifting to cool feedback. Two or more rounds of cool feedback are recommended.
6. Members can pass if they have nothing new to say. They can also agree with, ditto, add to, or build on something that someone else has said or give feedback that is completely different.

Warm feedback

- Endorses or values without praising.
- Is nonjudgmental and specific to the work.
- Provides the perspectives/points of view and beliefs of the reviewers.
- Focuses on importance, relevance, connections, usefulness, applicability, and possibilities.

  Examples:

  "You can also address _____ with _____."

  "This could also be combined with _____."

  "This might allow other readers to understand _____."

  "If you included _____, you could also _____."

Cool feedback

- Includes no negative judgments.
- Focuses on questions and confusions.
- Helps uncover the perspective/point of view and beliefs of the author.
- Elicits clarification by promoting thinking.

  Examples:

  "I wonder if you might . . ."

  "I don't understand . . ."

  "Why did you . . .?"

  "Could _____ have a negative effect on _____?"

  "I'm struggling to see how this . . ."

As you can see, the focus in this set of learning experiences is twofold. It is intended to both develop students' ability to be reflective about others' and their own work, and at the same time engage in the writing process.

Implications for Evaluating, Creating, and Revising Curriculum

When evaluating or creating curriculum, it is important to ensure that

• The learning experiences or lessons communicate what students will do, why, and the evidence the teacher will have of student learning.

• Lessons or clusters of learning experiences strongly align to the standards.

• Different types of lessons—content, process, and disposition— have been included.

The following two examples illustrate what learning experiences would look like if they were designed to address these criteria. The first example, shown in Figure 6.3, is an excerpt from the Fire Island, New York, curriculum. Here are the related unit standards:

RI.3.1   Ask and answer questions to demonstrate understanding of a text, referring explicitly to the text as the basis for the answers.

RI.3.4   Determine the meaning of general academic and domain-specific words and phrases in a text relevant to a *grade 3 topic or subject area.* [emphasis in original]

RI.3.6   Distinguish their own point of view from that of the author of a text.

W.3.1   Write opinion pieces on topics or texts, supporting a point of view with reasons.

W.3.5   With guidance and support from peers and adults, develop and strengthen writing as needed by planning, revising, and editing.

Figure 6.3

TYPES OF LEARNING EXPERIENCES — ELEMENTARY EXAMPLE

Learning Experiences	Type
Students **refer to the texts** they have been reading to **create a list** of **problems** *facing the Brazilian rain forest.* RI.3.1	Process/ Content
Students • **Define the terms** politics, economics, and ecology using information from the texts they have been reading about the rain forest. • **Check and clarify their definitions** using the online dictionary wordcentral.com; *make revisions to their definitions.* • **Provide examples** that *illustrate each word.* • **Classify problems in the rain forest** as *political, economic,* or *ecological.* RI.3.4	Process/ Content
Students • **Create a list of questions** that they have *about problems facing the rain forest.* • **Find and read a nonfiction article** *to answer their questions.* • Meet in small groups to **discuss and answer any remaining questions.** • **Use additional nonfiction text** *to clarify any contradictions or clarifications,* and **add to their answers.** RI.3.1	Process/ Content
Students • **Write their point of view** about the problems facing the rain forests and what can be done about them, and **create a list of details to support their point of view.** • **Read** *"All About the Rain Forest: Saving the World's Rain Forests,"* by Karen Fanning (2011), **and write** down the **author's point of view** and **list** the **details the author uses** *to support her point of view.* • **Create a "hat" chart** *to compare the author's point of view and use of supporting details with their own.* RI.3.6	Process/ Content
Students • *Examine language used by authors when sharing their opinion* by **revisiting the nonfiction articles they read to create a list of "strong" words that the authors used when sharing their opinion.** RL.3.4	Process
Students • **Revisit their written point of view and list of reasons to write a draft of their opinion piece** on how to take care of the rain forest. W.3.1, W.3.5	Process
Students • **Share their writing with a partner and use a checklist to give each other verbal feedback** on their written pieces. • **Complete a written reflection** *on whether the advice offered by their partner was helpful and how they might use it.* • **Make revisions to their pieces** based on partner feedback. W.3.5	Process/ Disposi- tions

The second example, shown in Figure 6.4, is an excerpt from a high school unit of study on homeostasis. (The same criteria apply regardless of content or grade level.) Here are the unit standards for the second example:

RST.9-10.7   Translate quantitative or technical information expressed in words in a text into visual form (e.g., a table or chart) and translate information expressed visually or mathematically (e.g., in an equation) into words.

5.3b   Feedback mechanisms have evolved that maintain homeostasis. Examples include the changes in heart rate or respiratory rate in response to increased activity in muscle cells, the maintenance of blood sugar levels by insulin from the pancreas, and the changes in openings in the leaves of plants by guard cells to regulate water loss and gas exchange.

In Figures 6.3 and 6.4, you can easily see by the coding that the learning experiences describe what the students will do, why, and the evidence the teacher has of student learning, and they ensure that the tasks are strongly aligned to a standard. The examples also include content, process, and metacognitive learning experiences, as evidenced by the labels in the second column. We should note here that if content, process, and dispositional standards have been carefully identified and arranged throughout the year, before the design of the assessments and learning experiences, and if steps have been taken to ensure alignment to these standards, these different types of lessons will naturally be part of the curriculum. This process of coding and labeling can then easily be copied when teachers are working to design curriculum and can be completed unit by unit as units are designed.

The process becomes slightly more difficult when evaluating a published or existing curriculum, primarily because the format is usually full lesson plans, often with more lessons than can actually be taught. Working in one

Figure 6.4

TYPES OF LEARNING EXPERIENCES—SECONDARY EXAMPLE

Learning Experiences	Type
Students • **Find and list <u>examples</u> of internal (genetic) and external** (nutrition, physical activity, mental health, environmental exposure) *factors that influence homeostasis; <u>identify and label</u> those that can be controlled and those that cannot.* 5.3b	Content
• <u>**Conduct and write**</u> **a lab report of an experiment** that *examines the body's response (breathing rate and pulse) to changes in physical activity.* 5.3b	Process/Content
• **View examples of feedback loops and explanations** that illustrate *the relationship between external factors and homeostasis;* in small groups <u>**discuss**</u> *how the written information has been translated into feedback loops.* 5.3b, RST.9-10.7	Process/Content
• **Create a <u>class</u>** *definition of negative and positive feedback* **based on their examination of the samples and explanations.** They <u>**color-code**</u> the *positive and negative feedback in each of the examples.* 5.3b, RST.9-10.7	Process/Content
• **Complete a <u>written response</u> in which they reflect** on *how the use of a feedback loop affected their understanding of homeostasis and include remaining questions.* 5.3b, RST.9-10.7	Disposition/ Process
• Work in groups to **draw a <u>diagram</u> that shows the feedback loop** examined during their experiment; <u>**color-code**</u> the *negative and positive feedback within the system.* 5.3b, RST.9-10.7	Process/Content

district to integrate a reading series into the curriculum, we faced the challenge of too many lessons, many of which were not strongly aligned and all written in very elaborate lesson plan formats. The team used the chart in Figure 6.5 (see p. 132) to analyze and select lessons to include in the curriculum.

We began with the unit description and then identified the standards that were taught and assessed, along with key words that identified the main idea of the standard. From there we identified the lessons that were moderately or strongly aligned to the standards for the unit and that focused on the student as the learner.

Figure 6.5
LESSON-ANALYSIS CHART

Unit Description	Standards	Lessons
Unit 3: Nature's Impact *Who's really in control?* Students understand how their world is affected by nature. They analyze different texts and how they convey information about the impact of nature on humans. At the end of the unit, they write an essay persuading people to be prepared.	RL.4.1 (use evidence, make inferences) RL.4.3 (describe character, setting, event using details) RI.4.1 (use evidence, make inferences) RI.4.3 (explain events, procedure using details) RI.4.6 (compare/contrast first- and secondhand account) SL.4.3 (identify reasons and evidence) W.4.1 (opinion writing)	Earth Science Lesson Topic: "Hurricanes" • Analyze the text • Explain scientific ideas • Use photos as primary sources First- and secondhand accounts of Katrina T39 • Compare accounts T193 • Use graphic features T262

Note: T indicates Teacher's Edition.

The following shows how information from the original analysis was reworked. The name of the main text appears first as the organizer for the related learning experiences. The learning experiences then include applicable resources from the reading program, including text, lessons, and materials (and, if applicable, the page numbers where they can be found—for example, "T93" stands for "Teacher's Edition, page 93"); a description of what students will do, why, and how; and standard code to ensure alignment.

"Hurricanes," by Seymour Simon

Students

• **Read the nonfiction text taking note of *how the author uses pictures, diagrams, and text to explain why hurricanes occur*** *and how they affect people.* They participate in a <u>small-group</u> <u>discussion</u>, with each member <u>sharing</u> something he or she learned from the text.

- **Reread the text and record the *different ways in which hurricanes affect people*** on a <u>two-columned chart</u>. RI.4.3

"Recovering from Katrina"

Students

- **Read the newspaper account of Katrina and record information** that *confirms information from the nonfiction text* in the second column of the <u>two-column chart</u>.
- **Use their <u>chart</u> to discuss how the *explanations*** *were similar to and different from each other.* T93, RI.4.6

Once the teachers completed their analysis of the reading program, they focused on examining how they could include content, process, and dispositional learning experiences, and design new ones where the learning experiences fell short.

The process just described serves as an example of how to integrate new programs, meet state mandates, or integrate the best of past practice in a meaningful and purposeful way. The same intent is also evident in the previously described science learning experiences. The experiment in which students examine the relationship among breathing rate, pulse, and physical activity is one that is required by New York State for students who will take the state exam for the Living Environment course.

With the knowledge of how to address instruction in the curriculum, we can now turn to the materials and resources that support instruction—the focus of Chapter 7.

Summary: Instruction

Learning experiences and lessons are two ways in which to communicate what should be taught on a daily basis. Both of these structures have strengths and weaknesses that should be acknowledged and addressed so they are appropriately used as the basis of instruction. Either structure should include information about what students will do, why they will do it, and what the teacher will have as evidence of student learning. These lessons and learning experiences should be strongly aligned to the standards for that unit.

Curriculum includes learning experiences or lessons that address content, process, and dispositions. Content learning experiences focus on what students are learning, process learning experiences focus on the how, and learning experiences that address dispositions focus on the how and the why.

Tools and Activities for Evaluation, Design, and Revision

- **Identifying What, Why, and How**—This activity (see the examples in Figure 6.1) serves two purposes. It can be used to distinguish between the two formats in which instruction is communicated (lessons and learning experiences), and it can also be used to help teachers to identify what students will do, why they will do it, and the evidence they will have of student learning within lessons and learning experiences.

- **Coding and Labeling Learning Experiences and Lessons**—The codes used in this chapter to identify **what the students will do,** *why the student will do it,* and the <u>evidence of learning</u> (boldface, italics, and underlining) can be used in the design of curriculum or when identifying lessons or learning experiences. The process helps to ensure that this information is clearly conveyed to the teachers using the curriculum. Part of the coding process includes the identification of the standard aligned with the lesson or cluster of learning experiences. The labeling of lessons and learning experiences with "Content," "Process," and "Dispositions" can also be done during the design or revision process to ensure that units include these different types of lessons.

- **Lesson-Analysis Chart**—This simple chart (see the example in Figure 6.5) can be used during the revision process to identify quality lessons to include in the new curriculum. It helps to focus the identification of lessons based on the purpose they will serve in the revised unit of study.

✔ Checklist for Evaluation, Design, and Revision

☐ The learning experiences or lessons are written so they describe what the students will do, why they will do it, and what the teacher will have as evidence of student learning.

☐ The learning experiences or lessons are strongly aligned to the standards for the unit of study in which they appear.

☐ The learning experiences and lessons address content, process, and dispositions.

Resources That Support Instruction

"The Harry Potter unit," "the DNA lab," "the Twitter project," "the I Have a Dream activity"—teachers have often referred to units or other chunks of curriculum through the names of the resources they use, illustrating the excitement they have for sharing their favorite books, technology, and materials with their students. The passion teachers have for these resources shows how much they truly care about what they teach. Their enthusiasm transfers to their students and creates an energy of learning in the classroom.

Although we would like to believe these feelings occur solely because of the resource itself, that is probably not the only reason why students feel more engaged. It is more likely because of what the teachers ask students to do with the resource. Creating that match between what students do and the resources they use is the focus of this chapter. In a quality curriculum, learning experiences integrate quality texts, technology, and other materials in engaging yet purposeful ways.

Texts

Students read text for many reasons, including to

- Examine organizational structure.
- Determine the author's purpose.

- Examine word choice and meaning.
- Evaluate an argument.
- Determine relationships between ideas.
- Gather information.
- Challenge their own thinking.
- Practice reading skills.
- Explore different genres, styles, authors, and cultures.

Each reason may require a different type of text, so it is possible for students to be reading multiple texts at the same time but for different purposes. Often the reasons are clearly established in the standards chosen for the unit. Let's look at some examples that illustrate how standards indicate purpose and how the purpose influences the choice of text and how it is used in a learning experience.

Example 1

Standard: RI.2.10 By the end of the year, read and comprehend informational texts, including history/social studies, science, and technical texts, in the grades 2–3 text complexity band proficiently, with scaffolding as needed at the high end of the range.

Type of Text: Complex text as determined by

- Qualitative measures such as level of meaning, structure, language, and knowledge demand.
- Quantitative measures such as Lexile scores that determine such factors as number of words and sentence length.
- The match between reader and task based on factors such as cognitive capabilities, reading skills, motivation and engagement, prior knowledge and experience, and content and themes.

Learning Experiences: Students

- *Preview From Seed to Plant,* by Gail Gibbons, by **placing small sticky notes** next to the title, headings, and subheadings.
- **Turn the heading or subheading** of each section **into a question** and **write it on the sticky note to** *guide the reading of the text.*

- **Underline/highlight information** in order to *answer the question* created from the heading/subheading.

Example 2

Standard: RL.11–12.5 Analyze how an author's choices concerning how to structure specific parts of a text (e.g., the choice of where to begin or end a story, the choice to provide a comedic or tragic resolution) contribute to its overall structure and meaning as well as its aesthetic impact.

Type of Text: Text selected needs to have a unique structure, such as an unusual beginning or ending or a comedic or tragic resolution.

Learning Experiences: Students read *We Are All Completely Beside Ourselves,* by Karen Joy Fowler. As they read, they

- **Track their thinking** *(reactions, understanding of characters and events, shifts in thinking)* as the story unfolds, on sticky notes or in a journal.
- **Share their reactions to the author's choice** to *start the book in the middle of the story, and the impact that decision had on the story itself,* in small-group discussions.

Example 3

Standard: W.7.1 Write arguments to support claims with clear reasons and relevant evidence.

Type of Text: Text that illustrates an argument and how a claim is supported by reasons and evidence.

Learning Experiences: Students read the book *George Bellows: Painter with a Punch,* by Robert Burleigh. The students

- **Read and discuss** the story *to develop an appreciation of George Bellows and his artwork.*
- **Identify the characteristics of the text** that *identify it as an argument* and **contribute to a class list,** *focusing on the inclusion and evaluation of an opposing point of view.*

- **Reread the text, and use different-colored <u>sticky strips</u> to** *identify the different points of view.*
- **Use their strips to <u>write sentences</u>** *showing the connection between opposing viewpoints* (e.g., Some people think _____, but _____).

Example 4

Standard: Colorado Career and Technical Education (CTE), Architecture and Construction Cluster, Design and Pre-Construction Pathway

DPCP 01. Technical Skills:
Use the technical knowledge and skills required to pursue the targeted careers for all pathways in the career cluster, including knowledge of design, operation, and maintenance of technological systems critical to the career cluster.

DPCP.01.01 Read, interpret, and use technical drawings, documents, and specifications to plan a project.

DPCP.01.01a Interpret drawings in project plans.

Type of Text: Floor plans of a wide range of quality

Learning Experiences: Students work in small groups to interpret a floor plan that they find on the Internet. They
- **Identify the *key elements of a floor plan* by creating a <u>list</u> of** what they notice about the plan.
- **<u>Share</u> their list to construct a <u>class checklist</u> of** *a quality plan.*
- **Use the checklist to <u>write an *evaluation* of the plan,</u>** *identifying how it incorporates the criteria and how it could be improved.*

In each of the examples, the characteristics of the text were identified from the standard and then the text was chosen because it exhibited those characteristics. Specifically,

- *From Seed to Plant* was selected because it exhibits the attributes of text complexity.

- *We Are All Completely Beside Ourselves: A Novel,* by Karen Joy Fowler, was selected because of its unusual structure.

- *George Bellows: Painter with a Punch,* by Robert Burleigh, was selected because it presents an argument.

- *Floor plans* were selected because they include specifications for planning a project.

Although these choices seem straightforward, we can learn a lot about choice of text through these examples, including how to address common misconceptions that often influence and limit the texts teachers use in their classrooms.

In the 2nd grade example, teachers chose the text *From Seed to Plant,* by Gail Gibbons, because it met the criteria for text complexity. The adoption of the Common Core State Standards or similar standards has led to some confusion as to what "text complexity" actually means and when students should read complex text. Unfortunately, text complexity has often been translated to mean a Lexile or other qualitative score. As shown in the description of the characteristics of the text, text complexity also includes qualitative features and meeting the demands of the reader and the task. In addition to the Lexile level, *From Seed to Plant* includes text features that students can use as a strategy for understanding the text. The text therefore meets not just one of the criteria for text complexity but also the other two because it has structural characteristics that can be used to meet the demands of the task. Many quality texts have been pushed aside because they are not of the "correct" Lexile score. Yet these texts, because of qualitative measures or how they are being used, may actually be complex text and more worthwhile to read.

In some cases concern over text complexity has also incorrectly led to the use of complex texts instead of varied levels of text, even though we know that students improve as readers when they have plenty of opportunities to read text at their own level. Before asking students to read *From Seeds to Plant,* teachers could have them practice the reading strategy of using text features to comprehend nonfiction texts with a text at their reading level. Once students had plenty of practice with text at their

reading level, they then could apply their reading strategies to more difficult texts.

We Are All Completely Beside Ourselves was chosen because of its
unique structure: it begins in the middle. However, many other contemporary as well as classical works of literature also have an unusual
beginning or ending, or a comedic or tragic resolution that would meet
this criterion; examples include *Defending Jacob* by William Landay, *My
Sister's Keeper* by Jodi Picoult, and Shakespeare's *Hamlet, Othello,* and
Macbeth. With such diverse choices, a text cannot be chosen based solely
on structure. In this case, *We Are All Completely Beside Ourselves* sits in a
unit with the following organizing center:

Unit Title: Humanity

Essential Question: What does it mean to be human?

Big Idea: Students understand that the parameters of what it
means to be human are not defined by all in the same way.

We Are All Completely Beside Ourselves is serving two purposes: it meets
the criterion of unusual structure, and it explores the ethical debate of animal rights in a unique way. In many units, teachers choose a text because it
can serve two purposes. It can be read for enjoyment and still be analyzed
for the author's use of language; it can be read to learn specific content
and still be used to analyze the author's use of evidence in making a claim.

This concept of two purposes is particularly important in content
areas where teachers feel there simply isn't enough time to cover the
content and read an outside text. For example, using a chapter from *The
Immortal Life of Henrietta Lacks* by Rebecca Skloot in a high school science class allows students the opportunity to use their scientific knowledge of cells as they read about and engage in the bioethical debate about
cell ownership. In a high school social studies classroom, students can
read an excerpt from *The Warmth of Other Suns* by Isabel Wilkerson and
compare it to other secondary and primary sources that capture the times

and experiences of African Americans who moved north and west during the Great Migration from the South.

In addition to illustrating how a specific text can be used, a quality curriculum also recommends alternative texts that will allow students to arrive at the end goal. For example, although *George Bellows: Painter with a Punch* is a good model for argumentative writing, a number of alternatives can serve as mentor text. These texts should be included in the curriculum so that teachers have quality options that they can choose from when thinking about the interests, needs, and learning styles of their students.

This idea of choice is in direct opposition to a common practice that asserts that all students in a given grade level or classroom should read the same text. Although this approach is helpful at times, many new opportunities emerge when students read different texts for the same purpose or reread a text in a different class or grade level for a new purpose. For example, teachers could use *George Bellows: Painter with a Punch* in any class—not only an ELA class—where students are writing arguments. An art teacher could also use it for examining George Bellows's artistic style or as a model for writing critiques. Confining a book to a specific grade level or class limits its use; rereading for different purposes promotes greater comprehension. Clearly identifying texts within the curriculum resources will promote this practice of multiple readings for different purposes by allowing all stakeholders access to information regarding what students are reading and why.

There are also times when it is best to describe the type of text but allow for a wide variety of quality, as seen in the learning experiences for architectural design. Here the goal was for students to access and evaluate floor plans for quality. In the real world, architects are not always handed a quality plan but rather need to know what to look for and what questions to ask in order to ultimately create a design plan. Although it would be advantageous to the students to have an exemplar to refer to while designing their own floor plan, the exemplar should not be their only model or necessarily the first plan they look at.

Technology

Examine these three standards and try to determine the grade level and content area to which they apply:

1. Students apply digital tools to gather, evaluate, and use information.

2. Students integrate and evaluate content presented in diverse formats and media, including visually and quantitatively, as well as in words.

3. Students read, view, and listen for information presented in any format (e.g., textual, visual, media, digital) in order to make inferences and gather meaning.

These standards come from different documents; the first is an ISTE standard, the second is a Common Core State Anchor Standard, and the third is from the American Association of School Librarians (AASL). Although each addresses the use of technology in slightly different ways, they all require that students use text, visual, media, and digital resources. These standards reflect the fact that, according to a survey by the Pew Research Center (Anderson, 2015; Perrin & Duggan, 2015), 87 percent of adult Americans use the Internet, 68 percent of Americans own smartphones, 45 percent own tablets, and 73 percent own a laptop or desktop computer, making it difficult to ignore the need to address technology in the curriculum.

I use the term *technology* here in the broadest sense of the word, to include the devices—computers, tablets, smartphones—that students use to access information, collaborate, and share what they have learned. Laptop computers and tablets are increasingly common, and schools vary in their policies regarding cell phone use and bring-your-own-device (BYOD) measures. The goal here is not to debate the merits and disadvantages of the devices or the related policies but rather to focus on what to include in the curriculum that will make the use of technology beneficial to students.

The general guiding principle around technology in the curriculum is to focus on how technology is a medium for learning rather than an end in itself (Pahomov, 2014). With that in mind, let's look at examples that illustrate the most common purposes that technology serves in the classroom: accessing information, collaborating and interacting, and presenting and publishing.

Accessing Information

We live in a world where we have immediate access to large amounts of information via the Internet, so the question in the classroom is not whether we should use the Internet to access information but rather how much information to include in the curriculum; in other words, do we tell students where to find information or do we let them find it on their own? The answer lies in how involved students are in the process of getting the information. The less involved they are, the more information needs to be included in the curriculum. The more involved they are, the less information needs to be included. Let's look at two examples to see exactly what this means.

Example 1

Students examine how speakers convey powerful messages by

- **Watching the video** *Be the Punchline* (Bass, Powers, & Michael Jr., 2014) **and working in small groups to complete a graphic organizer** *identifying* the message, details, and structure used by Michael Jr. *to make his point.*
- **Watching** Sam Berns's *My Philosophy for a Happy Life* **and** *identifying* his message, the details he uses to convey his message, and the structure used to support his point on the same graphic organizer.
- **Analyzing their graphic organizer** to create *criteria* for effective ways speakers use details and structure to make a point.

In this example, the students have a passive role in accessing information. The media have been preselected so the students can focus on analyzing the examples. Although students can find their own examples, it would be best for them to do so after establishing criteria for how speakers use details and structure to make a point.

The purpose for including these specific presentations is to identify examples of presentations and speeches students can view in order to analyze how a speaker uses structure and details to convey a message. Certainly other presentations and speeches could be used, and some teachers may opt to select their own; but—like some students—not all teachers will know how or where to look. Including this information in the learning experience gives teachers a starting point and gives students models to examine. In cases such as this one, including a specific website is particularly helpful in learning experiences in which students are being introduced to an idea or concept, practicing a specific skill, or evaluating an example.

Students are most involved in accessing information when conducting research on a topic of their choice. When students are choosing a topic, it is not feasible to offer all of the possible sources of information. What will be helpful to students are learning experiences that teach them to analyze the credibility of the sources they are examining, as well as learning experiences that show them how to use tools to organize, retrieve, and annotate their sources. Example 2 illustrates learning experiences focused on the process of collecting and organizing materials. In this case, students are collecting resources they will use for individual performance tasks that explore leadership.

Example 2

Students

- Explore the online tool Diigo by **watching an introductory video and browsing the site,** *taking note of what is easy to use and what is difficult;* they work in small groups to address the areas that were difficult.

- **Read 2–3 articles** from an open collection of resources they are interested in; *identify the relationship between the articles and the tags used to organize the articles.*

- **Contribute to a class list of tags** that could be used in *identifying articles about leadership.*

- **Research and <u>subscribe</u> to RSS feeds or SmartBriefs** that have the potential to include *articles on leadership*.
- **<u>Identify and tag</u> articles** to *include in the class Diigo library*.

Collaborating and Interacting

Another important role of technology in the classroom is that it allows students to collaborate and interact with each other, the teacher, and the general public in many different ways. In general, the choice of platform will depend on such factors as how many students will work together and the role the teacher will play in the interaction. The curriculum will need to identify appropriate platforms for interaction while the teacher identifies the collaborative groups or pairs and actively participates in feedback or discussions with her students, as shown in the following examples.

Example 1: Students use Storybird to create and illustrate original narratives.

In this example, Storybird is a specific platform that students can use to write and illustrate narratives. The decision to include this specific resource in the curriculum was based on several factors—namely, <u>Storybird</u>

- Is conducive to narrative writing because of its booklike structure.
- Includes a wide range of pictures that students can select from to reflect the storyline of their narrative.
- Can be configured as a closed network, allowing students to work together and receive feedback from their peers and teacher.
- Can be used for both process (the writing of the story) and publication (sharing the finished product).

Example 2: Students work in peer-editing groups using Google Drive to provide each other with feedback.

In this case, <u>Google Drive</u> is included as the tool of choice primarily because the school district has purchased Chromebooks that operate using Google programs. However, in addition to its availability, Google

Drive is a simple tool for the students and teacher to use for collaborating, documenting, and saving changes to work on a closed network.

In both of these examples, the tools are chosen based on their availability, ease of use, and appropriateness for the task. When students use collaborative or interactive tools for their own research, the description of a tool should be more open-ended, as in this example:

> *Example 3:* Students use an online tool such as SurveyMonkey or Twitter to conduct qualitative research for their inquiry project around the question *Is technology always good?*

In this case, the curriculum provides suggestions, but students are not limited to those choices. Students are expected to choose the interactive tool that they will use based on what they want to accomplish. They will need to set up their own network to collaborate with other members of their group and invite the teacher to participate or provide feedback.

These three examples illustrate only a small fraction of the technology that is available to facilitate student interaction. The possibilities are endless and continually changing, allowing students to survey, record, play, and create in new and exciting ways. To prevent getting lost in the myriad of choices and creating tasks that focus on the novelty of the tool, it is necessary to ask, *How is this tool or platform going to make the process more streamlined and make it easier for the students and teacher to work together?*

Presenting and Publishing

Like tools for collaboration, publication tools are numerous. In some cases, the collaboration tool is the same one that will be used for publication. The Storybird example is one such case; once the students complete their book, they can use Storybird to publish it for others to see.

Not all tools, however, will lead directly to publication. One platform may be needed for collaborating and a second for sharing the finished product. In these cases, the curriculum will either need to identify a tool for publication or leave it to student choice. Once again, the purpose will determine when a task should contain a specific tool or when the choice should be left open-ended. Let's look at two examples to determine what should be considered when making this decision.

> *Example 1:* Students choose one of the global issues featured on the United Nations website, http://www.un.org/en/globalissues/. After conducting research on the issue as a whole and focusing on a case study of how the issue affects a specific community, students write and submit a proposal for an awareness campaign. The class chooses one of the proposals and carries out the plan using the appropriate media and technology to reach their target audience.

In this performance assessment, the use of technology and appropriate tools is contingent on many factors. Limiting student choice would change the entire assessment. In this case, students would benefit from a series of learning experiences that feature the analysis of different media used for awareness campaigns, and the tools available for creating them.

> *Example 2:* Students create a LinkedIn page to establish an online professional presence.

In this task, the tool for publication is identified. Although other social media sites can be used for business networking, LinkedIn is the largest in the world. If the intention of the teacher is to provide graduating seniors with the opportunity to learn how LinkedIn works, it does not make sense for the choice of tool to be open-ended or for a different tool to be used. If the task were different—for example, create an online portfolio showcasing your accomplishments over the last four years—students could determine the specific platform to use. They could use video, photography, and graphics on a variety of different platforms, depending on the message and materials they wished to share.

Selecting technology for a curriculum should be done with full understanding of the terms of agreement, including matters related to security, privacy, and ownership. For example, Twitter requires an e-mail address, and LinkedIn has an age limit. Although both are public forums, they can be limited to select viewers. Research into different tools should be done before inclusion in the curriculum, so teachers can use the tool with confidence that it complies with school regulations and are clear about what steps need to be taken so students can use the tool safely.

Materials

This final category includes graphic organizers, models and exemplars, student checklists, primary sources, common templates, protocols, and other materials that support the learning experiences for the unit. The number of potential materials could be overwhelming and result in an unwieldy document if not properly managed, so the policy of "less is more" should definitely be applied when determining what to include. Here are some questions to consider when selecting or evaluating resources:

• *Is the resource an integral part of a learning experience?* If a learning experience refers to a specific protocol, organizer, photograph, or other resource, the resource should be included in the curriculum. For example, consider this learning experience:

> Students examine the painting *Harvest Time* by Grandma Moses and describe life in a rural community.

Because this learning experience references a specific painting, the painting should be readily available for teachers to use with their students. If the learning experience simply referenced the artwork of Grandma Moses—for example, "Students examine the paintings of Grandma Moses and describe life in a rural community"—it would be sufficient to include a website where the paintings could be found.

• *Does this resource include a process that will be repeated in subsequent units?* Processes that are likely to be repeated throughout the year as a regular routine include discussion protocols, procedures for lab experiments, steps for analyzing primary sources, and checklists for group work. In such cases, the guidelines and other supporting tools, such as rubrics, checklists, and reflection sheets, should be included in the unit where the process is introduced and then, depending on frequency of use, in subsequent units. For example, in this learning experience, students are introduced to a discussion protocol:

> Students participate in a Socratic seminar in which they discuss the essential question *What is more constant than change?*

If students engage in a Socratic seminar on a regular basis, in every unit, it is sufficient to include the protocol once. If the seminar occurs sporadically, it would be beneficial to include the protocol whenever it is used. In either case, because a specific protocol has been identified, it would be helpful to have the steps outlined in an easily accessible document.

• *Does this tool support school values?* Throughout this book, I have discussed ways to align curriculum to standards that reflect the district's or school's values. If a particular resource exemplifies these values, it should be consistently referenced and used throughout the curriculum. For example, if a district has decided to focus on fostering student thinking, they may be working with Thinking Maps (Hyerle, 2009). Thinking Maps consist of eight visual tools that are used for different cognitive functions. A teacher may choose to use a frame of reference circle map so that students can identify what they know about the causes of the Civil War, what has influenced their understanding, and the questions they have. The frame of reference circle map has been specifically chosen for this diagnostic task so the teacher can determine not only what students know, but also how reliable that information is, based on where it came from. Because fostering student thinking is a districtwide focus, the frame of reference circle map will appear in multiple curricula and will be used throughout the year; however, it should still appear in the curriculum the first time it is used, for easy accessibility.

Although purpose underlies the selection of texts, technology, and materials, it is important to also demonstrate cultural competency when selecting these resources. Cultural competency is the ability of a system to work effectively in cross-cultural situations (Goode & Dunne, 2004). As it relates to the choice of resources, cultural competency means being culturally aware of the students you work with and ensuring that the resources are representative of who they are or will expose them to cultures different from their own. A culturally aware curriculum will include resources that address, in an unbiased way, the religions, races, and cultural practices of the students, as well as those who are different from them.

Implications for Evaluating, Creating, and Revising Curriculum

A wealth of resources is available to teachers through the Internet and through programs purchased for schools, so whether evaluating a curriculum to determine if it should be purchased or revised or creating a new curriculum, the challenge is not only what should be included but also how to limit what is included.

The common theme throughout this chapter for determining what to include is purpose: what purpose will the text, technology, or resource serve in the curriculum? The identification of appropriate resources can occur simultaneously as learning experiences are being evaluated or created, as described in Chapter 6.

A quality curriculum includes learning experiences that identify what the students will do, why they will do it, and the evidence of student learning. The purpose for choosing a particular resource is identified in the description of why students will complete a task, making it simple to identify the necessary resources at the same time. Consider the following examples:

> *Example 1:* Students examine photographs from the *New York Times* photo essay *Poverty's Palette* and write a description of what life was like in the South during the Great Depression.

In this example, the images provide background information on what life was like in the South during the Great Depression. The pictures have a very specific purpose and should be easily accessible to the teachers who wish to use them; therefore, they should be included in the curriculum.

> *Example 2:* Students read the article "Alabama Pardons 3 'Scottsboro Boys' After 80 Years" by Alan Blinder (2013) and use key details from the article to write a summary of the events that occurred and their implications for today.

In this learning experience, the purpose of the account is twofold: to provide information to students and to have students use key details to write a summary. The article selected needs to meet these criteria. A primary source document that focuses on reaction to the trial's outcome could not be used for these purposes. Although it may be appropriate for the next learning experience, a narrative account of someone's feelings might not be the best for determining what happened at the trial and its implications 80 years later.

> *Example 3:* Students complete a double-bubble map to compare the Scottsboro trial with the trial of Tom Robinson in *To Kill a Mockingbird.*

In this example, the double-bubble map is used for comparison. This Thinking Map is included as part of the learning experience because it is structured to be used for mirrored analysis. Although a Venn diagram might be an alternative for some and can certainly be used for mirror analysis, it is a tool better suited for math and science. Because the double-bubble map is specifically identified in the learning experience and has a specific purpose, it would need to be included as a resource.

Using purpose to determine what should be included in the curriculum will help simplify the process of choosing resources. It may also reveal a resource better suited for another purpose within the curriculum. It is conceivable that teachers might use a portion of a classroom textbook or anthology in a way other than the one prescribed by the publisher.

In addition to determining what to incorporate in the curriculum, it is just as important to identify a way to limit and manage the resources included. This effort becomes particularly challenging when the curriculum is being implemented, for this is when teachers will adjust existing resources and find additional resources that they wish to include. It is important to have a system in place for managing these resources. One suggestion is to put in place a vetting process for reviewing resources before including them in the curriculum. The system can include a person or group responsible for reviewing materials based on an established set of criteria. This process will help to ensure the inclusion of quality materials with distinct purposes and help to eliminate resources that do not fully meet the purposes of the learning experiences or that duplicate existing materials. A second way to manage additional resources is by creating a folder or site on the district's network where teachers can upload and tag materials that others may use, similar to teacherspayteachers.com or other sharing sites. Because this approach allows for the inclusion of more materials, the folder or site would also need to be managed so that it does not become overwhelming.

Summary: Resources

Texts should be chosen for the curriculum based on the purpose or purposes they serve. This could mean that the same text is read for multiple reasons or that students read multiple texts at the same time because the purpose for reading is different. In some cases, it is not necessary to specifically identify a text. The curriculum can offer a selection of texts that meet the same criteria or describe criteria so students can select their own.

The guiding principle for determining what technology to include in the curriculum is to focus on the result and not the device itself. In general, technology is used to access information, to collaborate or interact with others, and to publish or share. The need to identify specific websites and platforms depends on the level of student involvement in the task. The more open-ended the task and the more involved the students are in the task—as when students engage in a self-selected, inquiry-based performance assessment—the less information needs to be included in the curriculum. Specificity is necessary when specific models, exemplars, websites, and tools are shared to introduce an idea or concept, used to practice a specific skill, or evaluated as models.

Materials include tangible products such as graphic organizers, models and exemplars, student checklists, primary sources, common templates, and protocols that are needed to engage in the unit's learning experiences. As learning experiences clearly communicate why students are completing a specific task, materials are selected because students will need them to accomplish the task.

A quality curriculum includes not only a process for the careful selection of quality resources but also a procedure for ensuring access to additional quality resources as the curriculum is being implemented.

Tools and Activities for Evaluation, Design, and Revision

• **Example Analysis: Analyzing Standards for Text Features—** These examples (beginning on page 137) can be used as models for choosing texts to meet a specific purpose. The text purpose and features are first extracted from the standard, and then appropriate texts are identified that address the purpose and features.

• **Example Analysis: Technology Integration—**This activity involves evaluating sample learning experiences. The first step is to identify the purpose of the learning experiences as described by *why* students will engage in the task. The second step is to determine how technology is used to achieve the purpose identified in the learning experience.

• **Guiding Questions to Analyze Resources—**The following three questions can be used to guide the review of resources when considering whether they should be included in the curriculum:

    – Is the resource an integral part of a learning experience?

    – Does this resource include a process that will be repeated in subsequent units?

    – Does this tool support school values?

✔ Checklist for Evaluation, Design, and Revision

☐ Texts, technology, and resources have been chosen because they meet a specific purpose as set out in the standards and learning experiences for the unit.

☐ Processes are in place for both the selection and limitation of texts, technology, and resources to include in the curriculum.

Success with Your Curriculum

Throughout this book I have suggested attributes to consider when examining or creating curriculum and have illustrated these attributes through many examples. In this concluding chapter, I present some final thoughts about what to consider for the successful implementation of your curriculum.

Easy Accessibility

A quality curriculum is easily accessible to teachers and other educators who use it. As you may have noticed, I have not recommended a specific format that should be used to house a curriculum. The reason is because there is no generic, one-size-fits-all format. What is most important is that the format should work for a variety of different types of users.

Although less of an issue than in the past, the first decision that many districts need to make is whether the curriculum should be paper, web based, or both. There may be economical, logistical, or other reasons that will greatly affect the outcome, but in all three cases, I suggest a layered approach, with each layer building upon the next so the curriculum can be used in different ways for different audiences.

The first layer of the curriculum should be short, succinct descriptions of the various units. These descriptions can easily be written by combining the essential question and the big idea with a description of what the students read, write, or create within the unit. The following is an example from the curriculum that was created by Amaris Scalia and Dawn Whelan when I worked with the North Rockland School District in New York in designing their curriculum:

> **Unit 1:** A Healthy Me. *How healthy am I?* Students understand that learning about exercise, food and nutrition, and healthy habits will help them evaluate and make decisions about living a healthy life. In this unit, students use their knowledge of informational texts to read and identify criteria for what makes people healthy. They use their criteria to write an evaluation of their own health and identify a step to become even healthier when answering the question *How healthy am I?*

> **Unit 2:** 20 Questions. *Why ask questions?* In this unit, students explore how asking questions can help them to understand the world around them. They learn to use questions as a way of making sense of different genres, including folktales, poetry and songs, and biographies and other forms of nonfiction. As a result, the students develop questions to interview a person in their life and write a biography sharing what they learned.

> **Unit 3:** Around the Town. *What defines a community?* Students learn that people in different communities share common characteristics but have features that make them unique. In this unit, students read nonfiction texts about rural, suburban, and urban communities and a variety of literature set in these communities. Students create a trifold brochure for new families that identifies common characteristics of all communities, and how and where they can be found locally.

> **Unit 4:** Animal Investigators. *Who shares our Earth?* In this unit, students understand that they share the planet with many different kinds of animals. Students learn how text features can be used to identify important details about different animal groups.

They use their understanding to create their own nonfiction books about an exotic animal that they will share with kindergarten students preparing for a trip to the zoo.

Unit 5: What's the Point? *What's the point?* Students understand that authors write for different purposes and that understanding an author's purpose will help them interpret the story or information presented. In this unit, students explore authors who write to inform, persuade, or entertain. They will use their knowledge of author's purpose to create an ad for a book they want to convince others to read.

These short descriptions can be shared with parents at back-to-school night or posted on the school's website. They provide just enough information so that the reader understands what students are learning about, what they will do, and why. Sometimes these unit descriptions contain a time frame (e.g., weeks 1–6), or they are linked to a curriculum map that identifies the number of weeks on a calendar. As discussed in Chapter 1, the length of a unit should be based on need and not a predetermined amount of time because units vary in their time requirements.

This overview should be linked to a standards-analysis document, as shown in Chapter 3 (see Figures 3.1 and 3.2). The standards-analysis document is the blueprint for the curriculum; not everyone needs or is interested in the rationale behind the placement of the standards for the curriculum, but the information should be accessible to anyone who wants it. Some parents, particularly those who are educators themselves, want to know the specific skills that are being taught and when, so they can better support their child at home. Some teachers will want access to the blueprint so they can see the big picture behind the placement of skills; others will view the blueprint and quite frankly become overwhelmed with the numbers. In any case, it should be available for those who want it.

The second layer of the curriculum is made up of the individual units. In a web-based program, links can connect the descriptions to the units. In a paper document, the fully developed units may follow the overview. Regardless, each unit contains the essential question, big idea, standards, assessments, and learning experiences. Many schools use Understanding by Design or a similar template to house their units of study. For example, Figure 8.1 illustrates what Unit 1 from the 2nd grade curriculum would look like in a standards-based design template. The unit appears in its entirety in Appendix A.

As you can see, the unit incorporates the considerations discussed in this book as they would apply to an individual unit. The specifics of how the Healthy Me unit addresses the attributes are described below in relation to the checklists that appear at the end of each chapter.

- ☐ The organizing center is articulated through the title, *A Healthy Me*; the essential question, *Am I healthy?*; and the big idea, *Students understand that learning about exercise, food and nutrition, and healthy habits will help them evaluate and make decisions about living a healthy life.*

- ☐ The organizing center for the unit of study is the idea that people make decisions that affect their health.

- ☐ The organizing center aligns to one of the values of the school: to engage students in integrated units of study that strongly align to the standards.

- ☐ The organizing center supports student learning by engaging students in the authentic task of evaluating their own health and creating a plan for improving it.

- ☐ The tasks are strongly aligned to the standards identified in the unit, and all standards that have been identified are taught and assessed in the unit, as evidenced by the coding throughout.

- ☐ The standards chosen for this first unit reflect important 2nd grade skills. For example, asking and answering *who, what, where, when, why,* and *how* questions is a fundamental skill for 2nd graders.

- ☐ The assessments used to measure student learning are congruent with the standards being measured. For example, students are asked to write an evaluation, which is an appropriate way to measure student writing.

Figure 8.1
HEALTHY ME UNIT

Stage 1—Desired Results

Essential Question: Am I healthy?	**Big Idea:** Students understand that learning about exercise, food and nutrition, and healthy habits will help them evaluate and make decisions about living a healthy life.

Guiding Questions

Content Questions

- What do humans need to grow and maintain good health? 5.3a

Process Questions

- How can asking and answering questions help me learn about being healthy? R.2.1
- How does making connections help me better understand what I read? RL.2.11
- How do individual paragraphs support the main idea? RI.2.2
- How do I express my opinion in writing? W.2.1
- How can I support my opinion with reasons that come from my experiences and books I have read? W.2.1, W.2.8

Metacognitive Questions

- What did you learn that was helpful in evaluating your own health?
- What were some of the reading strategies you used to help make sense of the stories and informational texts you read?

Standards

Reading Literature

RL.2.1   Ask and answer such questions as *who, what, where, when, why,* and *how* to demonstrate understanding of key details in a text.

RL.2.11 Make connections between self, text, and the world around them (text, media, social interaction).

Reading Informational Texts

RI.2.2   Identify the main topic of a multiparagraph text as well as the focus of specific paragraphs within the text.

Writing

W.2.1   Write opinion pieces in which they introduce the topic or book they are writing about, state an opinion, supply reasons that support the opinion, use linking words (e.g., *because, and, also*) to connect opinion and reasons, and provide a concluding statement or section.

W.2.8   Recall information from experiences or gather information from provided sources to answer a question.

(continues)

Figure 8.1
HEALTHY ME UNIT (continued)

Stage 1—Desired Results *(continued)*

Standards *(continued)*

NYS Elementary Science Core Curriculum

5.3   Describe the factors that help promote good health and growth in humans.

5.3a   Humans need a variety of healthy foods, exercise, and rest in order to grow and maintain good health.

5.3b   Good health habits include hand washing and personal cleanliness; avoiding harmful substances (including alcohol, tobacco, illicit drugs); eating a balanced diet; engaging in regular exercise.

Stage 2—Assessment Evidence

Diagnostic Assessment: Students write a response to the essential question *Am I healthy?* The teacher examines student responses for understanding of content and ability to state an opinion and support it with reasons. W.2.1

Formative Assessment Opportunity: Students read a variety of articles and nonfiction text about nutrition, exercise, and healthy habits. As they read, they write the main focus of each paragraph in the margin of the article, and at the end they identify the main topic of the text (RI.2.2). Students use information that they learn to complete a "notes booklet" that answers these questions on individual pages:

- Who are the people who help me stay healthy? RI.2.1
- What do I need to do to stay healthy? RI.2.1
- Where can I practice healthy habits? RI.2.1
- When do I need to practice healthy habits? RI.2.1
- Why is it important to be healthy? RI.2.1
- How can I be healthy? RI.2.1

Teachers will use students' responses to determine their understanding of main ideas and how well they are able to answer questions using the text. Teachers provide students with feedback on their notes so students can add or revise their information before writing their evaluation.

Performance Task: Students write an opinion piece answering the essential question *Am I healthy?* In their opinion piece (W.2.1), they

- Explain why they think they're healthy or not.
- Supply reasons that support their opinion.
- Use information that they learned about nutrition, exercise, and habits. W.2.8
- Use words and phrases and descriptive language related to nutrition, exercise, and healthy habits. RI.2.4, L.2.5
- Use linking words to connect their opinion and reasons.
- Provide a concluding statement in which they set a goal for improving their health.
- Follow conventions for standard grammar and spelling. L.2.1

Students draft, self-assess, and revise, using a student-friendly rubric or checklist (with teacher support as needed). W.2.5

Figure 8.1

HEALTHY ME UNIT (continued)

Stage 3—Learning Plan

Learning Activities*

Students

- **Complete a T-chart** *identifying the 5 Ws and H—who, what, where, when, why, and how—*after reading books such as *Dragon Gets By* and *Gregory the Terrible Eater.* RL.2.1

- **Use highlighters to identify** *what is similar and what is different between the two stories.* RL.2.11

- Read several articles on healthy habits—food, exercise, and behaviors. For each article, students **record the main topic of each paragraph on a flow map** to *identify the main idea of the article.* RI.2.2

- Review articles and information on Kidshealth.org and *use text features to determine the most important information.* Students will **complete a chart in which they name each article, the text features they examined, and what they learned.** RI.2.5

- Read stories that express opinions about foods—e.g., *Green Eggs and Ham;* they *identify the opinion being expressed and reasons used to support the opinion* **by creating a picture and quote** for the character expressing the character's opinion. W.2.1

- **Create lists of what they have learned** about nutrition, exercise, and healthy behaviors; **highlight the information** they can use to *support their evaluation.* W.2.7, W.2.8

- **Write down the steps they followed to write their evaluation** and participate in a class **discussion** in which they share, *What was easy/difficult about writing it?*

Suggested Resources

Stories

- *Gregory the Terrible Eater* (Mitchell Sharmat, José Aruego, and Ariane Dewey)
- *Dragon Gets By* (Dav Pilkey)

Informational Text

- *Good Enough to Eat: A Kid's Guide to Food and Nutrition* (Lizzy Rockwell)

Suggested Technology Integration

MyPlate (new food pyramid)
http://www.choosemyplate.gov/

Kid's Health
http://kidshealth.org/

* The coding in this section (boldface, italics, underlining) indicates **what students will do,** *why they will do it,* and the underline{evidence of learning}.

Source: From 2nd Grade Curriculum by Amaris Scalia and Dawn Whelan, North Rockland School District. Reprinted with permission.

☐ The unit clearly identifies and appropriately uses diagnostic, formative, or summative assessment.

☐ The diagnostic assessment is a response to the essential question *Am I healthy?* The teacher examines student responses for understanding of content and for the ability to state an opinion and support it with reasons.

☐ Formative assessment is used to monitor student learning. Assessment activities identify opportunities for teachers to monitor student understanding and provide students with descriptive feedback. They include creating the nonfiction text features book, completing the notes booklet, producing story maps, and writing drafts of the final evaluation.

☐ The performance task, which asks students to write an evaluation of their own health, is an integral part of the unit that produces as well as measures learning. It exemplifies the criteria for a quality task because it measures the most important learning as articulated in the organizing center, is congruent and strongly aligned to the unit standards, and brings together the diagnostic and formative measures.

☐ The performance task also includes a rubric that can be used for instructional and evaluative purposes (this rubric appears in Chapter 5, Figure 5.3). The rubric would be linked to this template so it is easily available to the teachers.

☐ The learning experiences are written so they describe what the students will do, why they will do it, and what the teacher will have as evidence of student learning. (In this example, that information has been coded as described in Chapter 6.)

☐ The learning experiences include content lessons addressing healthy habits; process lessons that focus on reading, writing, and vocabulary; and lessons focusing on metacognition, such as asking students to evaluate their own health and reflect on the writing process.

☐ Texts, technology, and resources have been chosen because they meet a specific purpose as set out in the standards and learning experiences for the unit. The learning experiences call for specific texts, technology, and resources that are identified in the Suggested Resources column.

The final layer in the curriculum consists of all of the resources that support the implementation of the unit. The assessment descriptions should be linked to student directions and materials, as well as any rubrics and checklists that will be used to guide the learning process and evaluate the final result. The learning experiences should also link to the materials and resources identified in their description. If a calendar or learning plan has been developed as a guideline for pacing, that should be linked as well.

A quality curriculum will make information and resources readily available to accommodate different users while allowing all users to guide their students to the same outcome. In addition to the grade-level teachers, the curriculum is now readily available to all teachers who support students in different capacities so they, too, can make informed decisions about their classroom practice. Special-area teachers such as art and music teachers may wish to link their curriculum to the time periods, events, people, literature, and concepts their students are studying in other classes. The physical education teacher may want a better understanding of the metacognitive strategies used in other classes so he can apply it to his own lessons. The English teacher may want to know what scientific concepts might lend themselves to topics that include controversial issues. An ESL department may wish to develop a curriculum that directly links to the English language arts curriculum. The special education teacher may want to know the skills being taught in specific units so that she can best support her students in using these skills. The possibilities are endless, but at least possible, given easy access to the curriculum.

Quality Professional Development

A quality curriculum is supported by quality professional development. Although the curriculum document should stand on its own, successful implementation requires opportunities for teachers to come together to learn about the thinking behind the curriculum, to make connections to their current practice, and to share their experiences during the implementation process. Here are some examples of what that might look like:

- A team of teachers come together to write the curriculum. The teachers represent different buildings and grade levels within the district, and they serve as liaisons, sharing information and receiving feedback from their colleagues as the curriculum is being written. Once a solid draft is complete, the curriculum is shared during grade-level meetings where teachers explore the rationale behind the curriculum, how it is organized, and how it could be used. This is followed by smaller grade-level sessions during the year, where teachers work with the curriculum, using it to plan and share strategies for instruction.

- A group of teachers evaluate their curriculum using the tools in this book. As a result, they identify an area of weakness, such as standards alignment or lack of assessments that produce as well as measure learning, and pursue an investigation into that area through their professional learning community. Based on their study, they make revisions to the curriculum, implement the revisions, and reflect on their changes.

- Teachers are examining the role of mindfulness in school. They participate in mindful practices as a community, read and view videos about mindful practices, explore the literature about the benefits of mindfulness, and try different strategies with their own students. As they do so, they make connections to their grade-level curriculum and include the practices they learn in their curriculum document.

- A grading and reporting committee has been formed to create a standards-based report card. Teachers examine research about the role of the report card as a tool to communicate information about achievement, growth, and student behavior and work habits. They collect and analyze various report cards used by other districts in reporting on these three areas. After deciding on an appropriate format, they use their curriculum to identify the report card descriptors, ensuring alignment between what they teach, how they assess it, and how they will report out on their students.

- A group of teachers is exploring strategies for differentiating instruction to meet the needs of all learners in their classrooms. In determining specific strategies, they examine the standards for the unit they will be teaching and the learning experiences that have been designed to address these standards. Based on this information, they identify how they can differentiate the content, process, or product yet meet the same goals.

The professional development in each of these schools has a different focus and takes place in a different way. However, all of these schools have something in common: the curriculum is an integral part of the process, not separate or an afterthought. By making the curriculum part of the process, teachers will be able to make connections among the many areas they are responsible for and make purposeful decisions about what happens in their classrooms.

Connection to Student Work

A quality curriculum is connected to student work. The final and most important key to ensuring a successful curriculum is analyzing it through the examination of student work. The protocol in Figure 8.2 (see p. 166), developed by Learner-Centered Initiatives, is designed to accomplish two goals: (1) to determine student needs and (2) to make revisions to tasks within a curriculum. This protocol is unique because it does not assume that if students demonstrate an area of weakness, it's because they did not learn the information or were unable to use a skill. Rather, it raises the following question: *Was the area of weakness demonstrated in the student work a result of the task itself or a lack of opportunity to learn and practice the necessary skills or information?*

To illustrate its impact, let's use the protocol with the following example of student work. The work is the result of a unit in which students examine the role of oral language in communicating the culture of a people, particularly the Iroquois American Indians. Students write a narrative that they will share orally, following the tradition of the Iroquois, at a local Iroquois cultural center.

The first step of the protocol is to read the specific directions for the task:

> **Task Description:** Students write a narrative as an Iroquois American Indian. In their piece, the students
> - Introduce themselves.
> - Explain their role in the Iroquois.

Figure 8.2
PROTOCOL FOR EXAMINING STUDENT WORK

Step 1: What was the purpose of the task? Review the directions and performance criteria to determine the intent of the task.

Step 2: What did the student(s) do? Read through the student work. In the margin of the student work, identify what the student knows and is able to do. The student need not have achieved mastery for the knowledge, skill, strategy, or behavior to be identified.

Step 3: Was there a match between what the student(s) did and the expectations for the task? Compare what the student knows and is able to do with the intent of the task. *If there is not a match, determine what kind of change needs to be made to the task so that there is.*

Step 4: What kind of support do the students need in order to demonstrate attainment of the expectations for the task? Determine what type of support the students will need in order to demonstrate understanding of the standards for the task. Consider how you will adjust subsequent lessons to assist students in reaching the standards.

Source: © 2011 by Learner-Centered Initiatives. Used with permission.

- Provide details about Iroquois society—for example, what did the Iroquois eat and why?
- Use the appropriate terms and language for describing Iroquois life.
- Provide a conclusion that summarizes the Iroquois experience.

The second step is to annotate the student work in relation to the expectations, taking note of what students know and are able to do. Figure 8.3 contains three examples that represent the diversity of what was reviewed and the teacher's annotation.

The third step, shown in Figure 8.4 (see p. 168), compares what students can do with the expectations, as delineated in the task description. When the student work is compared to the expectations, it is easy to see that all the students were able to incorporate information about how the Iroquois got their food and to some degree addressed the roles of men and women. What was not consistent was their development of Iroquois

Figure 8.3

STUDENT WORK AND TEACHER ANNOTATION

Student Work	What Does the Student Know? What Is the Student Able to Do?
Student 1 *I have just finished eating. I ate deer, corn, squash, beans, strawberries, sunflower seeds, and bread. The Iroquois call corn, beans, and squash "the Three Sisters." They are called "The Three Sisters" because they came from the body of the Creator, a woman. The sunflower seeds came from the sunflowers grown in the clearing. The bread was made by grinding the seeds into flour and making bread. The strawberries were picked from the forest just outside the clearing. I along with some of the other boys had to hunt ourselves. Sometimes we are made to hunt for ourselves so that we will have good hunting skills when we reach adulthood. All boys must learn how to hunt because men are the hunters in the tribe. The girls must learn how to farm because the women do the farming in the tribe. Tasks to be done in the village are divided equally between men and women. The men are in charge of the forests and the women are in charge of the clearing. Some of the foods that I enjoy eating that were not at the meal are wild mint, cherries, and plums.*	• Writes in first person. • Uses Iroquois terms: *Three Sisters, Creator.* • Describes the food of the Iroquois. • Describes how the Iroquois got their food. • Identifies himself as a boy. • Describes the role of men and women in Iroquois society.
Student 2 *Our main meal for the day is good and I am now finished eating. I am going to work in the clearing. The squash, beans, corn, and mushrooms are growing quite well there. I must gather some berries and nuts and find some wild plants. I will store them in a basket I made myself out of deerskin and moosehair. I will finish collecting the food in a short time. I must plant some dandelion and more mushrooms in the field. The men have already felled the trees so it will be an easy job. All of the men are out hunting for food and animal skins.*	• Identifies the food Iroquois eat. • Identifies where the food comes from. • Identifies how the basket is made. • Identifies what the men will do.
Student 3 *It is morning. The sun has just come up and Shining Sun is making today's main meal of corn soup, corncakes, and mushrooms. I, Shining Star, daughter of Shining Sun, am thinking about all I must do before the sun sets this day. There is much work to be done around the longhouse and in the clearing. Silver Stream, my grandmother, will also be working in the clearing, and Sharp Arrow, my grandfather, will be working in the forest with Falling Leaf, my father, and the rest of the men in the Bear Clan.*	• Uses names to identify herself and the other characters in the narrative. • Identifies the food that the Iroquois eat. • Provides a setting and time frame for the narrative. • Identifies the members of the clan. • Alludes to the role of men and women.

Figure 8.4

EXPECTATIONS AND STUDENT WORK

Expectations	Student 1	Student 2	Student 3
• Introduce themselves.	• Writes in first person. • Identifies himself as a boy.	• Writes in first person.	• Writes in first person. • Uses names to identify herself and the other characters in the narrative. • Identifies the members of the clan.
• Explain their role in the Iroquois.	• Describes the roles of men and women in Iroquois society.	• Identifies what the men will do.	• Alludes to the roles of men and women.
• Provide details about Iroquois society—for example, what did the Iroquois eat and why?	• Describes the food of the Iroquois. • Describes how the Iroquois got their food.	• Identifies the food Iroquois eat. • Identifies where the food comes from. • Identifies how the basket is made.	• Identifies the food that the Iroquois eat.
• Use the appropriate terms and language for describing Iroquois life.	• Uses Iroquois terms: *Three Sisters, Creator*.		
• Provide a conclusion that summarizes the Iroquois experience.			
• Other			• Provides a setting and time frame for the narrative.

identity and use of Iroquois language, and not evident at all were additional descriptions of elements of culture, oral language style, and a sense of closure.

Because our purpose is examining curriculum, the question to ask is, *What can we learn from the student work that we can use to revise the curriculum to improve student performance?* Although all three students wrote their stories in first person, only one made her character more relatable by providing a name for herself and the other characters in her story. This is information that would be helpful to all students and should be included in the curriculum, in both the directions and the learning experiences.

This student also set the context for her story by describing the setting. She begins her piece with two brief sentences: "It is morning. The sun has just come up." Although seemingly inconsequential, this bit of description would lend itself to incorporating aspects of oral tradition that were not addressed in the expectations at all but were stated as the focus of the unit. Oral tradition emphasizes imagery—particularly the kind that can be used for creating sound to describe sounds in nature. As the student continued, she could easily have described birds chirping and water flowing as part of this early-morning scene. If this was the teachers' expectation, the fact that no student included imagery or sound is an indicator that this information should be included in the expectations and in the learning experiences.

Another expectation that was addressed by only one student was use of appropriate terms and language. Students may have felt they addressed this expectation by including mention of specific foods, such as berries, nuts, wild plants, corn soup, and corncakes; but they did not include Iroquois language or terms. Improved task directions might have included a list of examples or a reference to resources used in class when discussing Iroquois terms. However, a cautionary note on this point is to include a variety of examples. Students interpret the listing of one or two examples to mean that those must be included—as illustrated by the fact that all three students addressed food as their example for the expectation "Provide details about Iroquois society." Food was the only aspect of Iroquois life that was explicitly identified in the directions. If the teachers were hoping for a wide range of examples, they should have suggested other options.

One expectation that was included but not addressed at all asked students to provide a summary of the Iroquois experience. One of many possible reasons for the omission might have been the clarity of the expectation. It reads more like an expectation for informational writing rather than for a narrative. This expectation would benefit from a revision that focuses on closure. Students could close their piece by describing the end of an activity or the end of a time of day, or by reflecting on an event.

With the comparison complete, the teachers could make the following changes to the expectations so all students have the opportunity to be successful:

> **Task Description:** Students write a narrative following the oral tradition of the Iroquois American Indians, to be performed at the Iroquois Cultural Center. In their story, they
>
> - Introduce themselves, following the Iroquois practice for naming.
> - Identify themselves as a child, a man, or a woman, and explain their role in Iroquois society from this perspective.
> - Provide details about one aspect of Iroquois society (e.g., food, family structure, games, religion).
> - Include an aspect of oral language such as imagery, creating sounds to describe sounds in nature, or rhythm or repetition in language.
> - Use the appropriate terms and language for describing Iroquois life (e.g., *Three Sisters, Creator, creation myth, matrilineal*).
> - Bring closure by ending the activity being described, describing the end of a certain time of day, or reflecting on an event.

Although these changes won't guarantee improvement, they certainly will make it more likely that more students will have the chance to succeed.

The changes bring greater specificity to vague language that may have come from translating standards into directions, and they clarify expectations for the teachers who designed the task.

Two things that will have a greater impact on student learning, however, are individualized and descriptive feedback to students and learning experiences that address student need. In the fourth step of the protocol (Figure 8.2), teachers brainstorm ideas for learning experiences that address areas of weakness discovered through the review of student work. The teachers can then include these learning experiences in the curriculum. For this particular task, they may want to develop learning experiences in which students further explore oral tradition, create an Iroquois vocabulary word wall, and examine mentor texts for descriptive writing— all of which would benefit students as they work on their next drafts.

In addition to providing feedback on the curriculum, student work that is collected and annotated can provide teachers with illustrations of different levels of performance and help them anticipate areas where students may need additional support. These examples can also be shared with students as models and exemplars for their own work.

Summary: Success with Your Curriculum

A quality curriculum is easily accessible to teachers and other educators who use it. It contains multiple layers that are linked to each other and provide varying degrees of information. These layers include unit descriptions, fully developed units, and supporting documents.

A quality curriculum is supported by quality professional development. Professional development should directly address the rationale, development, and use of the curriculum. The curriculum should also be included as part of other professional development to ensure a connection among curriculum, instruction and assessment, and related areas.

A quality curriculum is connected to student work. Student work is used to inform the curriculum, illustrate levels of performance, and determine student need.

Tools and Activities for Evaluation, Design, and Revision

• **Curriculum Checklist**—This checklist (see example beginning on page 158 of this chapter) can be used to evaluate individual units of study as well as the curriculum as a whole to ensure that the attributes of quality curriculum have been addressed.

• **Protocol for Examining Student Work** (Figure 8.2)—This protocol serves two purposes. First, it can be used to provide feedback on the curriculum by examining what students can do in relation to the expectations and then revising the expectations so all students have the opportunity to be successful. Second, the protocol can be used to iden-tify areas of student need so learning experiences can be developed to address those needs. These new learning experiences can also be incor-porated into the curriculum.

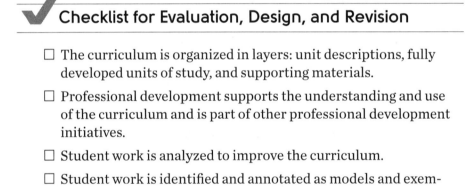

Checklist for Evaluation, Design, and Revision

☐ The curriculum is organized in layers: unit descriptions, fully developed units of study, and supporting materials.

☐ Professional development supports the understanding and use of the curriculum and is part of other professional development initiatives.

☐ Student work is analyzed to improve the curriculum.

☐ Student work is identified and annotated as models and exem-plars of the curriculum.

Epilogue

Those of you drawn to this book have the commonality of wanting to know what you can do to design, evaluate, or revise curriculum. Although your intended outcome—high-quality curriculum—may be the same, the reasons for your inquiry likely vary: new standards, new ideas about assessment, changing resources, state mandates, a desire to learn something new or understand curriculum from a different perspective. Whatever the reason, something prompted you to dig deeper into the curriculum design, evaluation, and revision process.

As an avid runner who came into the running scene in my early 40s, I felt a similar desire to learn more about my newly chosen sport. As I ran more consistently, in more races, and at further distances, I realized that simply getting out and running without a training plan or without paying any attention to the food I ate, the amount of water I drank, or the shoes I wore was not going to help me achieve the goals I set for myself.

My realization—that it is necessary to look at individual components, assess their quality, and improve upon them where necessary for overall success—applies to the curriculum evaluation and design process that I have set out in this book. My intention is to provide in-depth descriptions and tools for evaluating the individual parts of the curriculum to enable educators to determine what the curriculum does well and what it could do better, focus their efforts on the areas of greatest need, and improve the overall quality of the curriculum for student success.

As I prepared for my first New York City Marathon in 2014, I followed a carefully laid-out training plan, gave myself plenty of time to break in my sneakers, and experimented with different types and amounts of energy chews to find what worked for me. During the week leading up to the marathon, I ate the right balance of protein and carbohydrates while hydrating myself for the big day. The result was an awesome first marathon experience. The individual actions I took created a system (me) that worked well.

Making changes in the individual components—standards, assessments, and learning experiences—can have a strong positive effect on the curriculum. For example, ensuring that the curriculum-embedded performance assessment strongly aligns to the unit standards and organizing center can mean that students are engaged in assessments that produce and measure specific and deliberately chosen learning targets. However, if, in the process of aligning the curriculum-embedded performance task to the standards, the curriculum designers determine that one or more of the standards are not being assessed and do not either remove the standard from the unit or revise the performance task, the curriculum has not improved.

When one area of the curriculum is changed, it is vitally important to check how that change affects the whole. I learned this lesson the hard way when training for the 2015 New York City Marathon. I got sick three weeks before the marathon and could not run for a week. Instead of recovering and returning to the same training plan I had used the previous year, as was suggested in many of the articles I read, I tried to make up the time I had lost by running more. The result was not an awesome experience but, rather, an exhausting one. As I crossed the finish line, rather than feeling euphoric, I felt a great desire to lie down. I had failed to think about how the change in plan would affect the larger system.

A curriculum is a system made up of individual components. The entry point for the revision or development of curriculum will be based on the evaluation of each part of that system. However, it is important to realize and accept from the outset that the revision of one component will more than likely lead to the evaluation and revision of another component. For example,

- Revisions to address standards' emphasis and placement may lead to the examination of assessments to ensure alignment.

- Revisions of assessments may lead to the examination of learning experiences to ensure that they support students.

- Examination of learning experiences may result in revisions to ensure that they address content, process, and dispositions as well as articulate what students will do, why they will do it, and what the teacher will have as evidence of learning.

- Examination of assessments may indicate the need to design curriculum-embedded performance assessments that include diagnostic and formative assessment opportunities.

- Examination of formative assessment opportunities may reveal a need to better identify and describe the formative assessment process.

These are just a few of the connections that you may discover as you evaluate your curriculum. It is a process that takes time if your desired result is a high-quality curriculum that promotes student success.

In addition to providing tools and describing the evaluation and revision process, this book also explains what to consider when designing new curriculum. On occasion, something happens—standards change, new resources are purchased, or district priorities and values shift—that requires us to start from scratch. As I approach my third New York City Marathon, I am recovering from an injury and unexpectedly find myself starting from the beginning. My plan is to use my previous experiences as well as new knowledge and a professional trainer so that my next experience is better than my last. So whether your intention is to evaluate and revise or to design anew, the tools and processes included in this book can be used with your vast and personalized experiences to create a high-quality and meaningful curriculum for your students.

Appendix A

The following unit of study appears in part in Chapter 8 (see Figure 8.1), where it is explained using the attributes of quality curriculum. The full unit is contained here.

HEALTHY ME UNIT

Stage 1—Desired Results

Essential Question: Am I healthy?	Big Idea: Students understand that learning about exercise, food and nutrition, and healthy habits will help them evaluate and make decisions about living a healthy life.

Guiding Questions

Content Questions

- What do humans need to grow and maintain good health? 5.3a
- What are healthy habits? 5.3b

Process Questions

- How can asking and answering questions help me learn about being healthy? R.2.1
- How can I recount a story to determine its message? RL.2.2
- How do I describe the structure of the text? RL.2.5
- How does making connections help me better understand what I read? RL.2.11
- How do individual paragraphs support the main idea? RI.2.2
- How can I use what I know to determine the meaning of words and phrases in a text about health? RI.2.4
- How do pictures, diagrams, and text features help me locate important information and clarify what I read? RI.2.5, RI.2.7
- How do I express my opinion in writing? W.2.1
- How can I support my opinion with reasons that come from my experiences and books I have read? W.2.1, W.2.8
- How can working in a group help me do research? W.2.7, W.2.8
- What is the writing process, and how do I use it to strengthen my writing? W.2.5
- How do I share my opinion and ideas in a discussion? SL.2.1
- What can I learn about healthy habits from listening to others or from viewing films and other media? SL.2.2
- How do I communicate effectively to clarify my thoughts and ideas? W.2.1, SL.2.1, L.2.1
- How does the language I use affect how I communicate with others? L.2.5

Metacognitive Questions

- What did you learn that was helpful in evaluating your own health?
- What were some of the reading strategies you used to help make sense of the stories and informational texts you read?
- What steps did you follow to write your evaluation piece? What was easy/difficult about writing it?

Standards

Reading Literature

RL.2.1 Ask and answer such questions as *who, what, where, when, why,* and *how* to demonstrate understanding of key details in a text.

RL.2.2 Recount stories, including fables and folktales from diverse cultures, and determine their central message, lesson, or moral.

RL.2.5 Describe the overall structure of a story, including describing how the beginning introduces the story and the ending concludes the action.

RL.2.11 Make connections between self, text, and the world around them (text, media, social interaction).

Reading Informational Texts

RI.2.1 Ask and answer such questions as *who, what, where, when, why,* and *how* to demonstrate understanding of key details in a text.

RI.2.2 Identify the main topic of a multiparagraph text as well as the focus of specific paragraphs within the text.

RI.2.4 Determine the meaning of words and phrases in a text relevant to a *grade 2 topic or subject area.*

RI.2.5 Know and use various text features (e.g., captions, bold print, subheadings, glossaries, indexes, electronic menus, icons) to locate key facts or information in a text efficiently.

RI.2.7 Explain how specific images (e.g., a diagram showing how a machine works) contribute to and clarify a text.

RI.2.10 By the end of year, read and comprehend informational texts, including history/social studies, science, and technical texts, in the grades 2–3 text complexity band proficiently, with scaffolding as needed at the high end of the range.

Writing

W.2.1 Write opinion pieces in which they introduce the topic or book they are writing about, state an opinion, supply reasons that support the opinion, use linking words (e.g., *because, and, also*) to connect opinion and reasons, and provide a concluding statement or section.

W.2.5 With guidance and support from adults and peers, focus on a topic and strengthen writing as needed by revising and editing.

W.2.7 Participate in shared research and writing projects (e.g., read a number of books on a single topic to produce a report; record science observations).

W.2.8 Recall information from experiences or gather information from provided sources to answer a question.

Speaking and Listening

SL.2.1 Participate in collaborative conversations with diverse partners about *grade 2 topics and texts* with peers and adults in small and larger groups.

    a. Follow agreed-upon rules for discussions (e.g., gaining the floor in respectful ways, listening to others with care, speaking one at a time about the topics and texts under discussion).

    b. Build on others' talk in conversations by linking their comments to the remarks of others.

    c. Ask for clarification and further explanation as needed about the topics and texts under discussion.

SL.2.2 Recount or describe key ideas or details from a text read aloud or information presented orally or through other media.

Language

L.2.1 Demonstrate command of the conventions of standard English grammar and usage when writing or speaking.

    c. Use reflexive pronouns (e.g., *myself, ourselves*).

    d. Form and use the past tense of frequently occurring irregular verbs (e.g., *sat, hid, told*).

    f. Produce, expand, and rearrange complete simple and compound sentences.

L.2.5 Demonstrate understanding of word relationships and nuances in word meanings.

    a. Identify real-life connections between words and their use (e.g., *describe foods that are spicy or juicy*).

NYS Elementary Science Core Curriculum

5.3 Describe the factors that help promote good health and growth in humans.

5.3a Humans need a variety of healthy foods, exercise, and rest in order to grow and maintain good health.

5.3b Good health habits include hand washing and personal cleanliness; avoiding harmful substances (including alcohol, tobacco, illicit drugs); eating a balanced diet; engaging in regular exercise.

Stage 2—Assessment Evidence

Diagnostic Assessment: Students write a response to the essential question *Am I healthy?* The teacher examines student responses for understanding of content and ability to state an opinion and support it with reasons. W.2.1

Formative Assessment Opportunity: Students work in small groups (SL.2.1) to create a nonfiction text features book (W.2.8) about healthy foods, using information from a variety of sources including text and media presentations (SL.2.5). Each page of the book will share information about the major food groups using a text feature (RI.2.5, RI.2.7): captions, bold print, heading, subheadings, glossaries (RI.2.4), indexes, and diagrams. The teacher will use these books to determine student understanding of text features and healthy foods.

Formative Assessment Opportunity: Students read a variety of articles and nonfiction text about nutrition, exercise, and healthy habits. As they read, they write the main focus of each paragraph in the margin of the article, and at the end they identify the main topic of the text (RI.2.2). Students use information that they learn to complete a "notes booklet" that answers these questions on individual pages:

- Who are the people who help me stay healthy? RI.2.1
- What do I need to do to stay healthy? RI.2.1
- Where can I practice healthy habits? RI.2.1
- When do I need to practice healthy habits? RI.2.1
- Why is it important to be healthy? RI.2.1
- How can I be healthy? RI.2.1

Teachers will use students' responses to determine their understanding of main ideas and how well they are able to answer questions using the text. Teachers provide students with feedback on their notes so students can add or revise their information before writing their evaluation.

Formative Assessment Opportunity: Students work in small groups to read a fictional story in which the character learns about healthy habits. As they read, they use sticky notes to record who, what, where, when, why, and how information (RL.2.1). Students use their sticky notes to recount the story on a story map and identify the central message (RL.2.2, RL.2.5). They compare the information on their sticky notes about healthy habits in their story with the information in their "notes booklet." On the sticky notes students write the factual information and place a checkmark next to the information confirmed by their notes (RL.2.11). The teacher monitors students' understanding of the relationship between fact and fiction.

Performance Task: Students write an opinion piece answering the essential question *Am I healthy?* In their opinion piece (W.2.1), they

- Explain why they think they're healthy or not.
- Supply reasons that support their opinion.
- Use information that they learned about nutrition, exercise, and habits. W.2.8
- Use words and phrases and descriptive language related to nutrition, exercise, and healthy habits. RI.2.4, L.2.5
- Use linking words to connect their opinion and reasons.
- Provide a concluding statement in which they set a goal for improving their health.
- Follow conventions for standard grammar and spelling. L.2.1

Students draft, self-assess, and revise, using a student-friendly rubric or checklist (with teacher support as needed). W.2.5

Stage 3—Learning Plan	
Learning Activities*	**Suggested Resources**

Learning Activities*

Students

- **Complete a T-chart** *identifying the 5 Ws and H—who, what, where, when, why, and how—*after reading books such as *Dragon Gets By* and *Gregory the Terrible Eater.* RL.2.1
- **Use highlighters to identify** *what is similar and what is different between* the two stories. RL.2.11
- Read *Good Enough to Eat* **identifying the 5 Ws and H—***who, what, where, when, why and how—***on a graphic organizer.** RI.2.1
- **Create a T-chart** *showing the connection between the information* identified in *Good Enough to Eat* and *Gregory the Eater.* RL.2.11
- Read *Strega Nona* and ***use a story map to identify what happened*** at the beginning, middle, and end. RL.2.2
- ***Label the introduction and conclusion*** on their story map. RL.2.5
- Read *The Sweetest Fig* and **complete a story map that they will use to recount the story** with a partner, *explaining how the beginning introduces the story and the ending concludes the action.* RL.2.2, RL.2.5
- ***Discuss* the answer to the question** *What is the role of "magic food" in both stories to better understand the message of the story?* RL.2.1
- Read several articles on healthy habits— food, exercise, and behaviors. For each article, students **record the main topic of each paragraph on a flow map** *to identify the main idea of the article.* RI.2.2
- **Draw a picture and write a sentence for each tier-two word** *in order to understand its meaning.* RI.2.4
- **Define and classify words about health and nutrition** *in order to understand their meaning and relationship to one another.* RI.2.4
- *Identify different types of text features by* **completing a text-feature scavenger hunt using sticky notes.** RI.2.5, RI.2.7

Suggested Resources

Stories
- *Yoko* (Rosemary Wells)
- *Gregory the Terrible Eater* (Mitchell Sharmat, José Aruego, and Ariane Dewey)
- *Cloudy with a Chance of Meatballs* (Judi Barrett and Ron Barrett)
- *How My Parents Learned to Eat* (Ina R. Friedman and Allen Say)
- *Dragon Gets By* (Dav Pilkey)
- *In the Night Kitchen* (Maurice Sendak)
- *Dim Sum for Everyone* (Grace Lin)
- *Green Eggs and Ham* (Dr. Seuss)

Informational Text
- "Nutrition" *(Kids Discover Magazine)*
- *What Happens to a Hamburger?* (Paul Showers and Edward Miller)
- *Good Enough to Eat: A Kid's Guide to Food and Nutrition* (Lizzy Rockwell)
- *Healthy Eating series* (Susan Martineau and Hel James)
- *Eat Your Vegetables! Drink Your Milk!* (Dr. Alvin Silverstein, Virginia Silverstein, and Laura Silverstein Nunn)
- *The Food Pyramid* (Christine Taylor-Butler)
- *Physical Fitness* (Dr. Alvin Silverstein, Virginia Silverstein, and Laura Silverstein Nunn)
- *Staying Safe* (Dr. Alvin Silverstein, Virginia Silverstein, and Laura Silverstein Nunn)
- *Exercise* (Liz Gogerly and Mike Gordon)
- *Healthy Habits* (Rebecca Weber)

Poems
- "Sick" (Shel Silverstein)
- "The Pizza" (Ogden Nash)
- "Bananas and Cream" (David McCord)
- "Chicken Soup with Rice: A Book of Months" (Maurice Sendak)

- Use a <u>T-chart</u> to *identify the type of text feature and information learned* about *nutrition, exercise, or healthy behaviors as a result of examining the text feature.* RI.2.5, RI.2.7
- Review articles and information on Kidshealth.org and *use text features to determine the most important information.* Students will **complete a <u>chart</u> in which they name each article, the text features they examined, and what they learned.** RI.2.5
- **Study diagrams** from Kidshealth.org and other websites that explain healthy habits; they **write <u>sentences</u> about what they** *learn from each diagram.* RI.2.7
- Read and *evaluate labels on cereal boxes* and **create a <u>list</u> of healthy cereals.** RI.2.5
- **Create a new healthy cereal and design the <u>box</u>** *using different text features to show why the cereal is healthy.*
- **Create their own <u>healthy plate</u>** *to show their understanding of MyPlate.* RI.2.7
- **Read and <u>draw a diagram</u>** based on the information in *What Happens to a Hamburger?* *to show their understanding of how the text feature communicates information.* RI.2.7
- **Record information that shows how they spend time; use a <u>chart</u>** *to share the information and identify different types of exercise.* RI.2.5
- **Listen to poems and <u>discuss</u>** *how the poems convey information about the authors' opinion on food.* W.2.1, SL.2.2
- Watch videos and **use criteria for *"most important" information* to <u>list</u> information** about healthy behaviors such as hand washing. SL.2.2
- Read stories that express opinions about foods—e.g., *Green Eggs and Ham;* they *identify the opinion being expressed and reasons used to support the opinion* <u>by</u> **creating a picture and quote** for the character expressing the character's opinion. W.2.1
- **Create <u>guidelines</u>** *for respectfully sharing and listening to opinions.* SL.2.1
- **<u>Discuss</u> their favorite foods,** *sharing opinions and reasons.* W.2.1, SL.2.1

Stories (Read Aloud)
- *Strega Nona* (Tomie dePaola)
- *Chato's Kitchen* (Gary Soto and Susan Guevara)
- *Too Many Tamales* (Gary Soto and Ed Martinez)
- *Everybody Cooks Rice* (Norah Dooley and Peter J. Thornton)
- *My Mom Loves Me More Than Sushi* (Filomena Gomes and Ashley Spires)
- *The Sweetest Fig* (Chris Van Allsburg)

Poems (Read Aloud)
- "Turtle Soup" (Lewis Carroll)
- "Eats: Poems" (Arnold Adoff and Susan Russo)
- "Boa Constrictor" (Shel Silverstein)

Songs
- "Dry Bones" (Traditional)
- "I'm Being Swallowed by a Boa Constrictor" (Traditional)

Suggested Technology Integration

MyPlate (new food pyramid)
http://www.choosemyplate.gov/

Nutrition Café
http://exhibits.pacsci.org/nutrition/nutrition_cafe.html

Kid's Health
http://kidshealth.org/

Little D's Expedition Games
http://www.nutritionexplorations.org/kids.php

- **Participate in a "taste test"** of healthy snacks, fruits, and vegetables, ***sharing verbally their opinions*** *about what tasted best and why.* W.2.1
- **Have a <u>discussion</u> about healthy habits with a partner** *in preparation for writing.* W.2.1
- **Create <u>lists</u> of what they have learned** about nutrition, exercise, and healthy behaviors; **<u>highlight the information</u>** they can use to *support their evaluation.* W.2.7, W.2.8
- ***Revise and edit <u>drafts</u> of their opinion pieces using checklists and teacher feedback.*** W.2.5
- **<u>Tell</u> "exercise" stories** *using past tense.* L.2.1b
- Examine and **<u>edit opinion pieces</u> looking to expand and rearrange simple and compound sentences,** and then *apply their understanding to their own writing.* L.2.1c
- **Look for reflexive pronouns in their writing; check against criteria** *for usage* and make revisions to their <u>drafts</u>. L.2.1c
- **Create a healthy <u>food collage</u>;** *use descriptive words* when identifying food. L.2.1c
- Listen to *Yoko* and **<u>discuss</u> the *different types of food people eat.*** 5.3
- **<u>Sort</u> foods into the correct *food groups*.** 5.3a
- **Search for, cut out, and glue pictures of healthy foods from a supermarket flyer into a <u>shopping cart</u>** *to demonstrate understanding of eating healthy.* 5.3b
- *Examine what is meant by "evaluation"* by **evaluating the choices made by different characters in the books that they read,** labeling a good choice and a bad choice, and giving advice for next time on <u>personal</u> whiteboards.
- **<u>Discuss</u> with a partner their own *health habits* using the same *evaluation*:** good choice, bad choice, and advice.
- **<u>Write</u> down the steps they followed to write their evaluation** and participate in a class <u>discussion</u> in which they share, *What was easy/difficult about writing it?*

---

* The coding in this section (boldface, italics, underlining) indicates **what students will do,** *why they will do it,* and the <u>evidence of learning</u>.

Source: From 2nd Grade Curriculum by Amaris Scalia and Dawn Whelan, North Rockland School District. Reprinted with permission.

Appendix B

The examples provided throughout this book illustrate how the attributes of quality curriculum can be addressed in different content areas. In this appendix, a 6th grade math unit is annotated to demonstrate how the attributes of quality curriculum apply to mathematics. The math unit is presented by attribute and explained using the checklist provided at the end of each chapter.

Consideration 1: Organizing Centers

Organizing Center

Unit Title: *Relationships in Real-Life Mathematics: Ratios and Proportions*

Essential Question: What relationships exist between numbers?

Big Idea: Students use their knowledge of multiplication and division to develop an understanding of ratio and rate language. They use this understanding to describe relationships, connect ratios and fractions, and solve real-world problems.

The organizing center is articulated through the unit title, the essential question, and the big idea. The focus of the organizing center for this unit transcends the content to the underlying conceptual understanding of how ratios and proportions are used to represent a relationship between two quantities. Thus, the organizing center for this unit of study is the concept that ratios and proportions are used to demonstrate the relationship that exists between quantities and can be used to solve real-world problems.

Additional organizing centers for this curriculum include

- **Unit 2: Math for Every Day: Operations with Multidigit Numbers and Dividing Fractions.** *How can you be fluent in mathematics?* Students understand that the fluent use of addition, subtraction, multiplication, and division of whole numbers and fractions will help them to solve problems that they encounter every day.

- **Unit 3: Systems: Rational Numbers.** *Can a number be negative?* Students understand that the system of rational numbers includes negative numbers.

- **Unit 4: Solve for the Unknown: Expressions and Equations.** *How can a letter be a number?* Students understand that letters can be used to represent numbers in expressions and equations and that what they have learned about letters in math can be used to solve these kinds of problems.

- **Unit 5: Formulas: Area, Surface Area, and Volume.** *Is there a formula for math?* Students understand that expressions and equations can be used to solve for unknowns in area, surface area, and volume problems.

- **Unit 6: Analyzing Data: Statistics.** *What do the data say?* Students understand that statistical analysis includes identifying a question that can be answered with data, collecting and representing the data, summarizing the data, and relating the data to the original question.

Each of the units in this curriculum explores concepts that have been identified as critical areas in mathematics according to the Standards for Mathematical Content. These include

- Connecting ratios and rate to whole-number multiplication and division and using concepts of ratios and rate to solve problems.

- Completing understanding of division of fractions and extending the notion of number to the system of rational numbers, which includes negative numbers.

- Writing, interpreting, and using expressions and equations.

- Developing understanding of statistical thinking.

The organizing centers for this curriculum align to the values of the school: to <u>engage students in real-life applications</u> of mathematics and promote student use of the Standards for Mathematical Practice.

The organizing center supports student learning because <u>it is connected to authentic real-world learning.</u> In this unit of study, students are asked to find, explain, and solve a real-world problem of their choice using their understanding of ratios and proportions.

Consideration 2: Alignment to Standards

Content Standards
- **6.RP.1** Understand the concept of a ratio and use ratio language to describe a ratio relationship between two quantities.
- **6.RP.2** Understand the concept of a unit rate a/b associated with a ratio $a:b$ with $b \neq 0$, and use rate language in the context of a ratio relationship.
- **6.RP.3** Use ratio and rate reasoning to solve real-world and mathematical problems—e.g., by reasoning about tables of equivalent ratios, tape diagrams, double number line diagrams, or equations.

  ○ **6.RP.3a** Make tables of equivalent ratios relating quantities with whole-number measurements, find missing values in the tables, and plot the pairs of values on the coordinate plane. Use tables to compare ratios.

  ○ **6.RP.3b** Solve unit rate problems including those involving unit pricing and constant speed.

  ○ **6.RP.3c** Find a percent of a quantity as a rate per 100; solve problems involving finding the whole, given a part and the percent.

  ○ **6.RP.3d** Use ratio reasoning to convert measurement units; manipulate and transform units appropriately when multiplying or dividing quantities.

Standards for Mathematical Practice
- **MP.1** Make sense of problems and persevere in solving them.
- **MP.2** Reason abstractly and quantitatively.
- **MP.6** Attend to precision.

process standards

The tasks are strongly aligned to the standards identified in the unit. Both the content standards and the Standards for Mathematical Practice that have been identified are taught and assessed in the unit, as evidenced by the coding in the assessment descriptions and learning experiences.

Consideration 3: Standards Placement and Emphasis

	Unit 1	Unit 2	Unit 3	Unit 4	Unit 5	Unit 6
Ratios and Proportions Content Standards **6.RP.1** Understand the concept of ratios and use ratio language to describe a ratio relationship between two quantities.	X					
6.RP.2 Understand the concept of a unit rate a/b associated with a ratio $a{:}b$ with $b \neq 0$, and use rate language in the context of a ratio relationship.	X					
6.RP.3 Use ratio and rate reasoning to solve real-world and mathematical problems—e.g., by reasoning about tables of equivalent ratios, tape diagrams, double number line diagrams, or equations. a. Make tables of equivalent ratios relating quantities with whole-number measurements, find missing values in the tables, and plot the pairs of values on the coordinate plane. Use tables to compare ratios. b. Solve unit rate problems including those involving unit pricing and constant speed. c. Find a percent of a quantity as a rate per 100; solve problems involving finding the whole, given a part and the percent. d. Use ratio reasoning to convert measurement units; manipulate and transform units appropriately when multiplying or dividing quantities.	X					
MP.1 Make sense of problems and persevere in solving them.	X	X			X	X
MP.2 Reason abstractly and quantitatively.	X		X	X		X
MP.6 Attend to precision.		X			X	X

Note that the Standards for Mathematical Content, like other content-area standards, are designed so that the content is taught and assessed in one particular unit of study. When students revisit content standards, they do so in the context of new and related content. Therefore, the content standards naturally appear in one unit and are not revisited the same way as process standards are.

The Standards for Mathematical Practice, on the other hand, are process standards. The skills and habits of mind embedded within these standards are intended to be used throughout the year. They should be highlighted in units where students are taught specific strategies for addressing these standards. In this unit, students are taught strategies to

- **MP.1** Make sense of problems and persevere in solving them.
- **MP.2** Reason abstractly and quantitatively.
- **MP.6** Attend to precision.

These standards will be revisited, and the remaining Standards for Mathematical Practice will be highlighted as standards that are taught and assessed in other units.

Standards placement is carefully considered in mathematics, where new knowledge is based on previously learned concepts. A rationale for the placement of units across the year should be developed. In this curriculum, Ratios and Proportions was chosen as the first unit because it builds on students' prior knowledge of multiplication, division, and measurement.

The duration of each unit of study in a mathematics curriculum is based on need. Not all units require the same amount of time. The model unit provided here is designed to last six weeks because the concepts taught are new. Teachers must spend time making explicit connections to what students learned in 4th and 5th grade and to what they will be learning as 6th graders. A subsequent unit on area, surface areas, and volume lasts only four weeks because it extends what was learned in the previous unit about expressions and equations.

Consideration 4: Assessment Types and Purposes

The assessments used to measure student learning are congruent with the standards being measured. This attribute of quality applies in mathematics as it does in all other content areas. In the sample unit, the standards ask students to

- Describe a ratio relationship using ratio language.
- Solve real-world and mathematical problems in which they make sense of problems and persevere in solving them.
- Reason using tables of equivalent ratios, tape diagrams, double number line diagrams, or equations.
- Attend to precision when using rate and ratio language and identifying the solution.

The assessments for the unit are congruent with the standards because they consist of a variety of different types of product assessments in which students can demonstrate these understandings.

This unit includes multiple measures of student understanding. Students express their understanding of ratios and proportions by completing a multistep problem, finding and solving a problem in their own lives, and completing a unit test and a process assessment. The unit clearly identifies and appropriately uses diagnostic, formative, and summative assessments, focusing on assessment purpose rather than timing.

Diagnostic assessment. The problems included in the diagnostic assessment are designed to uncover student understanding of ratios and proportions as well as any misconceptions about these related concepts. The questions included in the diagnostic assessment are aligned to the foundational skills for the unit, which are taught in 4th and 5th grade.

Diagnostic Assessment

Students solve a series of multiplicative comparison problems (4.OA.A.2):

- Joseph wants to buy a frame for his new poster. The poster is 12 inches wide and 3 times as long. What size frame does he need?

- Your parents want to put a pool in the backyard. The width of the pool is 20 feet, and the pool is twice as long. Draw and label a diagram of the pool. Find its perimeter and area.

- Pam's room is 120 square feet. It is 12 feet long. Draw and label a diagram of Pam's room. What is its perimeter?

Students are given a series of problems in which they apply their understanding of fractions as division (5.NF.B.3):

- Catherine has 15 ounces of cookie dough. She wants to make 6 cookies. How many ounces of cookie dough should she use for each cookie so that they are all the same size?

- Paige wants to share her candy with 5 friends. She has 8 pieces of candy. How many pieces of candy can each friend have?

- William used 6 ounces of cheese on the pasta dinner he made for his friends. He had 4 plates of pasta. How many ounces of cheese did he use on each plate? Use a tape diagram to show your work.

Students are given a series of pictures and asked to describe the relationships they see and what the relationships have in common (6.RP.1, MP.1):

- A garden with 6 pepper plants and 30 tomato plants

- A calendar showing the month of April (30 days) with 5 days labeled as rain

- The United States flag (50 stars, 13 stripes)

Formative assessment. The formative assessment opportunities identify specific points in the unit that are advantageous to the formative assessment process, during which the teacher and students engage in ongoing exchange of feedback.

Column 1: Formative Assessment Opportunities	Column 2: Feedback
What opportunities has the teacher created for formative assessment?	*How does the teacher provide feedback or opportunities for peer feedback and self-reflection?*
Formative Assessment Opportunity:	
Exit Tickets	The teacher uses the exit tickets to
• Exit Ticket 1: Evaluating Ratio Statements (Illustrative Mathematics)	• Provide students with individual feedback.
The ratio of the number of boys to the number of girls at school is 4:5. There are 270 students at this school. For each of the following statements, explain whether the statement is true or false and why:	• Determine next steps for instruction. • Group students to address their needs.
a. The number of boys at school is 4/5 the number of girls.	
b. 4/5 of the students in the school are boys.	
c. There are exactly 30 more girls than boys.	
d. There are exactly 30 boys at the school.	
e. 5/9 of the students in the school are girls. **6.RP.A1**	
• Exit Ticket 2: Riding at Constant Speed (Illustrative Mathematics)	After receiving feedback, students have the opportunity to redo their problem and are given new problems to solve in which to apply the feedback.
Lin rode a bike 20 miles in 150 minutes. If she rode at a constant speed,	
a. How far did she ride in 15 minutes?	
b. How long did it take her to ride 6 miles?	
c. How fast did she ride in miles per hour?	
d. What was her pace in minutes per mile? **6.RP.2, 6.RP.3**	
• Exit Ticket 3: Diminishing Return (Insidemathematics.org, 2014)	
Maxine and Sammie have lawns that are the same size. Maxine can mow her lawn in 24 minutes, and Sammie can mow his	

lawn in 36 minutes. After how many minutes will Sammie have twice as much lawn to mow as Maxine? Maxine and Sammie have to also mow their parking strips that are the same size. Maxine can mow her parking strip in 6 minutes, and Sammie can mow his parking strip in 9 minutes. After how many minutes will Sammie have twice as much grass to mow as Maxine? **6.RP.3**

Formative Assessment Opportunity: Process Reflection

As students complete their exit problems, they reflect on the following questions:

- How were you able to make sense of the word problem?
- What steps did you take to solve the problem?
- How did you know they were the right steps?
- What did you do if you ran into trouble?
- How did you make sure your answer was accurate and precise?

The teacher reads students' responses to the process questions. She compares the students' perceptions with the work they completed on the exit tickets. The teacher uses this information to determine which strategies should be retaught and whether new strategies should be introduced.

Formative Assessment Opportunity: Performance Task Submission

Students submit a problem they have found that could be solved using ratios and proportions.

The teacher reviews students' submissions to determine whether students are able to identify real-world problems that show the relationship between numbers and could be solved using ratios and proportions. She provides students with feedback so that they may clearly articulate a real-world problem that can be solved using their understanding of ratios and proportions.

The first opportunity for formative assessment is the exit tickets. These problems have been identified as formative assessment opportunities because they align to the unit standards in such a way that the teacher can check for student understanding and adjust instruction before proceeding to a more complex understanding of ratios and proportions. These opportunities also begin the feedback process between teacher and students, where the teacher provides descriptive feedback that enables the students to revise their work and apply their understanding to new problems provided by the teacher.

In addition, when students solve multistep, real-world problems such as those found on the exit tickets, they have the opportunity to demonstrate the behaviors of a mathematician that have been explained through the Standards for Mathematical Practice. In this unit, the Standards for Mathematical Practice ask students to

- Be able to understand the problem, choose a method for solving the problem, and then self-correct if the method does not work or students realize that their solution is incorrect or unreasonable.

- Decontextualize the problem from the real-world situation and then contextualize it to check for reasonableness and ensure the accuracy of the answer as it relates to the initial situation.

- Attend to precision to ensure that their answers are properly labeled, particularly when the problem involves converting units.

The process reflection is another formative assessment opportunity that can be used to determine whether the students were aware of the processes they used for solving the exit ticket problems. The teacher can use the information from the exit tickets and the process reflection to provide students with individual feedback on their strategies as well as to address common issues and provide additional strategies through class lessons.

The final formative assessment opportunity in this unit prepares students for the performance task. Students share a real-world problem with the teacher, and the teacher provides feedback on whether the problem they have chosen for the performance task is one that demonstrates the relationship between two numbers and calls for the use of ratios and proportions in understanding and solving the problem.

The formative assessment opportunities within this unit provide students with feedback while it still can be used. It is important that the feedback students receive in mathematics does more than simply provide students with the correct answer; it is most effective when it identifies what the student was able to do, provides a question to prompt or deepen student understanding, and provides direction for solving the problem without directly giving students the answer. Descriptive feedback such as this can promote student understanding.

Summative assessment. The summative assessment is built off the formative assessment opportunities and can be used to determine what students have learned.

Summative/Performance Task

Students complete a multistep math task in which they work with a recipe to meet the needs of individuals who come into a bakery. As students complete the task, they are asked to

- Determine the ratio between ingredients. **6.RP.3**
- Change the amount of the ingredients based on the order (e.g., double the recipe). **6.RP.3**
- Explain ratios between old and new recipes. **6.RP.3.D, MP.6**
- Determine costs of ingredients. **6.RP.3**
- Determine increases in cost using tables and plotting the values on a coordinate plane. **6.RP.3**
- Determine the mileage traveled by different customers. **6.RP.3**
- Create equations to represent the problems. **MP.2**
- Create visual representations of the problems. **6.RP.3**
- Explain the process used to solve the problems. **MP.1**

Performance Task

Students find an example of how ratios are used to solve problems in the real world. They

- Explain the problem to be solved. **6.RP.1**
- Create an equation to represent the problem. **MP.2**
- Create a visual representation of the problem. **6.RP.3**
- Explain how ratios were used to solve the problem. **6.RP.3, MP.1**

Students will present their problems, solutions, and strategies in small groups. Students will have the opportunity to question one another to learn more about the different strategies presented by their classmates. Once all members of a group have had the opportunity to share, students will be asked to write a reflection on how mathematics presents itself in real life and how the different strategies and solutions might be helpful when they encounter new problems.

Other Summative Assessment: Ratios and Proportions Unit Test

The summative assessments for the unit are designed to measure student understanding of the big idea: *Students use their knowledge of multiplication and division to develop an understanding of ratio and rate language. They use this understanding to describe relationships, connect ratios and fractions, and solve real-world problems.* Each summative assessment—the on-demand performance task, the curriculum-embedded performance task, and the unit test—measures student understanding under different circumstances and therefore provides the teacher with a wealth of information on what the student knows and is able to do.

Consideration 5: Curriculum-Embedded Performance Assessments

The performance task, which asks students to find an example of how ratios are used to solve problems in the real world, is an integral part of the unit that produces as well as measures learning. It exemplifies the criteria for a quality task because it measures the most important learning as articulated in the organizing center, is congruent and strongly aligned to the unit standards, and brings together the diagnostic and formative measures.

The performance task also includes a rubric that can be used for instructional and evaluation purposes. The rubric for this performance task focuses on student understanding of ratios and proportions rather than solely on whether the student answer is correct. Its dimensions align to both the content standards for the unit and the Standards for Mathematical Practice.

	Wow!	Got It!	Almost There	Still Working
Understanding of Ratio and Unit Rate				
6.RP.A.1: Understands the concept of a ratio and uses ratio language to describe a ratio relationship between two quantities.	Uses ratio language and underlying concepts of multiplication and division to describe the relationships between two quantities.	Uses ratio language to describe ratio relationships as the comparison of two quantities.	Identifies a ratio as two numbers that are somehow related to each other.	Identifies a ratio as two separate numbers.
6.RP.A.2: Understands the concept of a unit rate a/b associated with a ratio $a{:}b$ with b not equal to 0, and uses rate language in the context of a ratio relationship.	Understands the concept of unit rate and how unit rates are connected to ratio; can describe the relationship between the two and each individually, using rate language.	Understands the concept of a unit rate associated with a ratio and can use rate language to describe unit rate as an expression of a ratio relationship.	Identifies a ratio or unit rate independent of each other but has difficulty explaining the relationship between the two.	Considers unit rate and ratio to be the same thing.
6.RP.A.3: Uses ratio and rate reasoning to solve real-world and mathematical problems—e.g., by reasoning about tables of equivalent ratios, tape diagrams, double number line diagrams, coordinate planes, or equations.	Analyzes a complex real-world problem using ratio and rate reasoning to determine the best strategy *(tables of equivalent ratios, tape diagrams, double number line diagrams, coordinate planes, or equations)* to solve for unit rate.	Solves a real-world problem for unit rate by applying a ratio strategy *(tables of equivalent ratios, tape diagrams, double number line diagrams, coordinate planes, or equations)* that demonstrates understanding of ratio and rate reasoning.	Solves a simple real-world problem using a ratio strategy *(tables of equivalent ratios, tape diagrams, double number line diagrams, coordinate planes, or equations)* to solve for unit rate.	Provides a realistic problem and identifies the unit rate or ratio, but the ratio strategy *(tables of equivalent ratios, tape diagrams, double number line diagrams, coordinate planes, or equations)* either is used incorrectly or is not evident.

MP.1: Makes sense of problems and perseveres in solving them.	Strategically makes a plan (explains the problem, organizes information), carries out the plan using multiple strategies (monitors, changes plan if necessary), and evaluates (checks) its success based on the problem.	Successfully makes a plan (explains the problem, organizes information), carries out the plan (monitors, changes plan if necessary), and uses a strategy to check the solution.	Makes a plan but may struggle with successfully carrying out the plan to arrive at a correct solution; work reflects attempts at self-correction, with errors.	Solves the problem without evidence of a plan and without attempting to self-correct or check the solution.
	Demonstrates perseverance and commitment to excellence by taking extra steps to ensure that the problem is solved correctly using ratio strategies.	Demonstrates perseverance by checking his or her work to make sure it is correct using an appropriate ratio strategy.	Demonstrates perseverance by completing the problem using the most familiar or easiest ratio strategy.	Completes the problem as quickly as possible.
MP.2: Reasons abstractly and quantitatively.	Uses the context of the real world to make sense of the problem, uses a ratio strategy to create an equation from the problem, and then checks the reasonableness of his or her answer within the context of the original problem.	Breaks apart the problem and uses a ratio strategy as a way to make sense of and solve the problem; returns to the problem to correctly identify and label his or her solution.	Pulls the numbers from the problem and uses a ratio strategy to solve it without paying attention to the original problem.	Uses numbers from the problem without noticing whether the numbers are the correct ones given the problem he or she is trying to solve; there may be an attempt to use a ratio strategy.
	Explains decontextualizing and contextualizing the problem as part of the reasoning processes.	Focuses on the ratio strategy as the primary way to make sense of the problem and explain his or her reasoning.	Explains the steps of the ratio strategy as his or her reasoning.	Reasoning is shared only through an attempt to use a ratio strategy; no written explanation is provided.

	Wow!	Got It!	Almost There	Still Working
MP.6: Attends to precision.	Correctly labels units of measure and symbols; solutions are correct.	Labels units of measure and symbols; solutions are correct.	Labels the most obvious units of measure and symbols; solution may or may not be correct.	Writes an answer with no evidence of labeling units of measure and symbols; solution may or may not be correct.
	Clearly explains his or her thinking throughout using precise ratio language and mathematical terminology.	Explains his or her thinking using ratio language.	Describes his or her thinking in general terms.	Explanation is a restatement of the problem; relies on the most basic math terms.

Consideration 6: Instruction

Students

- *Review their understanding of multiplicative comparison as a foundation for ratios* by **completing tasks such as identifying the fraction of shaded blocks or the fraction of cookies on a tray.**
- *Use multiple forms of ratio language and ratio notation* as they **read about or watch video clips about ratio relationships and then discuss and model the described relationships.** (6.RP.A.1)
- **Work in small groups to think of, describe, model, and share ratio relationships** from their own experience *to practice using ratio language to describe ratio relationships.* (6.RP.A.1, MP.6)
- **Read about or watch video clips** about situations that call for *establishing an equivalent ratio* and then **discuss and model the situations.** (6.RP.A.1)
- **Solve simple problems** of *finding one or more equivalent ratios.* (6.RP.A.1)
- **Use linking cubes to** *represent ratio relationships.* (6.RP.A.1)
- **Solve a problem of the day** in which they create ratios for a flower shop. (6.RP.A.1)
- **Find *values of quantities in a ratio*** when given different scenario cards that include the total desired quantity or when given the difference between the two quantities. For example, if the ratio of boys to girls in the school is 2:3, find the number of girls if there are 200 more girls than boys. (6.RP.A.1)
- **Use short descriptions to *illustrate ratios* using numbers, pictures, and words.** For example, if the number of chairs to people in the room is 2:1, show that ratio using numbers, pictures, and words. (6.RP.A.1)
- **Create tables** when given *two ratios to compare.* For example, if the ratio of pens to pencils is 2:1, would that be the same ratio as 6:4? (6.RP.A.3.A)
- **Create tables** to *understand that a ratio is the relationship between the amount of one quantity and the amount of another.* Then use this understanding to **solve problems** involving *mixtures and constant rates.* (6.RP.A.3.A, MP.1, MP.2)
- **Review their tables in small groups and discuss** *how the tables reflect what they know about addition and multiplication.* (6.RP.A.3.A)
- **Work with unit rate to write and explain the correct mix of paints** and *understand part-to-part and part-to-whole relationships.* (6.RP.A.3.A)
- **Work in small groups to create ratio tables** and then use them to **create double number lines** *in order to view and solve real-world problems.* (6.RP.A.3.A)
- **Solve problem sets of** *real-world problems* **using double number lines.** (6.RP.A.3.A, MP.1, MP.2)
- **Represent ratios in ratio tables, equations, and double number line diagrams** and **then represent those ratios in the coordinate plane** *in order to view and solve real-world problems.* (6.RP.A.3.A, MP.1)
- **Take a class walk around the schoolyard; set up a table and draw a graph to** *determine the relationship between the distance and speed of walkers* in their group. (6.RP.A.3.A, MP.1)
- **Work in small groups to identify the associated rate when given a ratio** *in order to understand ratio relationships.* (6.RP.A.2)
- Work with a series of real-world scenarios to **define and explain the *difference between the terms* rate, unit rate, *and* rate unit.** Students return to the scenarios and **identify the rate, unit rate, and rate unit.** (MP.6)

- **Use <u>representations and diagrams</u> to *determine the unit rate*** within the context of real-world rate problems. (6.RP.A.2, MP.1, MP.2)
- **Work through and <u>discuss problem sets</u>** that require expressing simple ratios as rates *using precise language* such as *"per," "for each," and "for every."* (MP.6)
- **Read the book** *If You Hopped Like a Frog* by David M. Schwartz. Then choose one of the scenarios presented in the book and read the corresponding explanation. Students use this information to **work in small groups to *solve the ratio problem* presented. Students present the problem and the *method* they used to solve the problem** during a <u>class gallery walk</u>. (6.RP.A.2, MP.2)
- **Solve unit rate <u>problems</u>** involving *unit pricing, constant speed, and constant rates of work.* (6.RP.A.3.B, MP.1, MP.6)
- **<u>Convert</u> different-sized standard measurement units** to *prepare for solving real-world problems with different units.* (6.RP.A.3.D)
- **Solve real-world <u>problem sets</u>** in which they *convert units.* (6.RP.A.3.D, MP.1, MP.2)
- **Plan for a class party by *comparing unit rate for items* using supermarket flyers.** They will <u>write a recommendation</u> of what to buy and where and why they should buy it. (6.RP.A.3.D)
- **<u>Conduct real-world simulations</u>** that *generate rates related to speed and work.* (6.RP.A.3.D)
- **Create <u>percent grids</u>** to *represent percentages.* (6.RP.A.3.C)
- **Use <u>percent grids</u>** to *represent real-world scenarios involving percent.* (6.RP.A.3.C)
- **<u>Write fractions as percents</u>** and *find a percent of a quantity in real-world contexts.* (6.RP.A.3.C)
- **<u>Read, interpret, and solve percent problems</u> using tape diagrams and double number line diagrams** or combinations of both explaining the *relationship between percent and ratio.* (6.RP.A.3.C, MP.1)
- **Read** *The Transcontinental Railroad.* Students will **work in small groups to solve problems** that were faced during the building of the railroad and *use their understanding of ratio and unit rate* to solve those problems. (6.RP.A.3, MP.1, MP.2, MP.6)
- **Solve the <u>problem of the month</u>,** First Rate, to apply their *understanding of ratio and unit rate.* (6.RP.A.3, MP.1, MP.2, MP.6)

The learning experiences are written so that they describe **what the students will do**, *why they will do it*, and what the teacher will have as <u>evidence</u> of student learning. The learning experiences are strongly aligned to both the content and the practice standards as indicated by the codes that appear at the end of each experience.

The learning experiences address content, process, and dispositions. Often, content learning experiences overlap with process and disposition learning experiences. For example, a lesson where students use representations and diagrams to determine the unit rate within the context of real-world rate problems requires students to make sense of the problem and determine the best approach for solving the problem (process), to use their understanding of unit rate to solve the problem (content), and then to persevere through the solving of a multistep problem where they may need to self-correct and check their answer (disposition).

Consideration 7: Resources That Support Instruction

Materials resources
- Grade 6 Mathematics Module 1 by EngageNY (2013). Available: https://www.engageny.org/resource/grade-6-mathematics-module-1

Web resources
- 6RP Evaluating Ratio Statements by Illustrative Mathematics (n.d.). Available: https://www.illustrativemathematics.org/content-standards/6/RP/A/1/tasks/2091
- Problem of the Month: Diminishing Return by Inside Mathematics (2014). Available: http://www.insidemathematics.org/assets/problems-of-the-month/diminishing%20return.pdf

Picture books
- *If You Hopped Like a Frog* by David M. Schwartz (1999). New York: Scholastic.
- *The Transcontinental Railroad: Using Proportions to Solve Problems* by Therese Shea (2007). New York: Rosen Publishing Group.

Texts, technology, and resources have been chosen because they meet a specific purpose as set out in the standards and learning experiences for the unit. The materials resources and technology resources give teachers choices on the types of problems they can provide for their students. Having a variety of resources will assist the teacher in differentiating instruction for their students, ensuring that all will have access to the content while working with problem sets most appropriate for their needs. The picture books have been integrated into specific lessons and should be available to all teachers if they choose to use them.

References

Anderson, M. (2015, October 29). Technology device ownership: 2015. Washington, DC: Pew Research Center. Retrieved from http://www.pewinternet.org/2015/10/29 /technology-device-ownership-2015/

Bass, M. (Director), Powers, M. (Producer), & Michael Jr. (Performer). (2014, August 24). *Be the punchline.* BassCreative.com. Available: https://www.youtube.com /watch?list=PLA9Tfcj6L1bLLq6I-7rnCl6Q7JizoS1oa&v=w2MORc0ZCo8

Beck, I. L., McKeown, M. G., & Kucan, L. (2002). *Bringing words to life: Robust vocabulary instruction.* New York: Guilford.

Berns, S. (Performer). (2013, December 19). My philosophy for a happy life. *TedX MidAtlantic.* Blueskymedia. Available: http://tedxtalks.ted.com/video/My-philosophy-for-a-happy-life

Bilton, N. (2013, September 15). Disruptions: Minecraft, an obsession and an educational tool [Blog post]. Retrieved from *New York Times,* Bits at http://bits.blogs.nytimes.com /2013/09/15/minecraft-an-obsession-and-an-educational-tool/?ref=education&_r=2

Black, P., & Wiliam, D. (1998). Assessment and classroom learning. *Assessment in Education: Principles, Policy & Practice, 5*(1), 7–74. doi: 10.1080/09695980050102

Blinder, A. (2013, November 21). Alabama pardons 3 "Scottsboro Boys" after 80 years. *New York Times.* Retrieved from http://www.nytimes.com/2013/11/22/us/with-last-3-pardons-alabama-hopes-to-put-infamous-scottsboro-boys-case-to-rest.html?_r=0

Blythe, T., Allen, D., & Powell, B. S. (1999). *Looking together at student work.* New York: Teachers College Press.

Brookhart, S. M., & Moss, C. M. (2014, October). Learning targets on parade. *Educational Leadership, 72*(2), 28–33.

Brookins Santelises, S., & Dabrowski, J. (2015). Checking in: Do classroom assignments reflect today's higher standards? [*Equity in Motion Series*]. Washington, DC: The Education Trust.

California Academic Content Standards Commission (CACSC). (2000). *History–social science content standards.* Sacramento, CA: California Department of Education.

Chingos, M. M., & Whitehurst, G. J. (2012, April 10). *Choosing blindly: Instructional materials, teacher effectiveness and the Common Core.* Washington, DC: Brown Center on Education Policy at Brookings. Available: http://www.brookings.edu/research /reports/2012/04/10-curriculum-chingos-whitehurst

Costa, A., & Kallick, B. (2000), *Discovering and exploring habits of mind.* Alexandria, VA: ASCD.

EngageNY. (n.d.). *Pedagogical shifts demanded by the Common Core State Standards.* Retrieved from https://www.engageny.org/resource/common-core-shifts

Fanning, K. (2011). All about the rain forest: Saving the world's rain forests. *Scholastic News: Inside the Rain Forest.* Retrieved from http://teacher.scholastic.com/scholasticnews /indepth/rainforest/rainforest.asp

Goode, T. D., & Dunne, C. (2004). Cultural self-assessment [*Curricula Enhancement Module Series*]. Washington, DC: National Center for Cultural Competence, Georgetown University Center for Child and Human Development.

Hyerle, D. (2009). *Visual tools for transforming information into knowledge.* Thousand Oaks, CA: Corwin.

Lorain, P. (2015, September 10). Brain development in young adolescents. Washington, DC: National Education Association. Retrieved from http://www.nea.org/tools/16653.htm

Martin-Kniep, G. O. (1999). *Capturing the wisdom of practice: Professional portfolios for educators.* Alexandria, VA: ASCD.

Martin-Kniep, G. O. (2000). *Becoming a better teacher: Eight innovations that work.* Alexandria, VA: ASCD.

Martin-Kniep, G. O. (2006, April). Assessing worthy outcomes. Presentation for the Assessment Liaisons Program, Albany, NY.

Martin-Kniep, G. O. (2008). *Communities that learn, lead and last: Building and sustaining educational expertise.* San Francisco: Jossey-Bass.

Marzano, R., Pickering, D., & Pollock, J. (2001). *Classroom instruction that works: Research-based strategies for increasing student achievement.* Alexandria, VA: ASCD.

McTighe, J., & Seif, E. (2014, Spring). *Teaching for understanding: A meaningful education for 21st century learners.* Retrieved from http://jaymctighe.com/wordpress/wp-content /uploads/2011/04/Teaching-for-Understanding.pdf

McTighe, J., & Wiggins, G. (2013). *Essential questions: Opening doors to student understanding.* Alexandria, VA: ASCD.

Moss, C., & Brookhart, S. (2012). *Learning targets: Helping students aim for understanding in today's lesson.* Alexandria, VA: ASCD.

National Governors Association Center for Best Practices (NGA Center) & Council of Chief State School Officers (CCSSO). (2010). *Common Core State Standards.* Washington DC: NGA Center and CCSSO.

National Governors Association Center for Best Practices (NGA Center) & Council of Chief State School Officers (CCSSO). (2010). *Common Core State Standards for English language arts and literacy.* Washington, DC: NGA Center and CCSSO.

New York State K–12 Social Studies Framework. (n.d.). Available: https://www.engageny.org /resource/new-york-state-k-12-social-studies-framework

Next Generation Science Standards (NGSS). (n.d.). *Get to know the science standards.* Available: http://www.nextgenscience.org/next-generation-science-standards

Next Generation Science Standards (NGSS). (2013). *Next Generation Science Standards: For states, by states.* Washington, DC: National Academies Press.

Nitko, A. J. (2001). *Educational assessment of students* (3rd ed.). Upper Saddle River, NJ: Prentice-Hall.

Pahomov, L. (2014). *Authentic learning in the digital age: Engaging students through inquiry.* Alexandria, VA: ASCD.

Perrin, A., & Duggan, M. (2015, June 26). *Americans' Internet access: 2000–2015.* Washington, DC: Pew Research Center. Available: http://www.pewinternet.org/2015/06/26 /americans-internet-access-2000-2015

Popham, W. J. (1999). *Classroom assessment: What teachers need to know* (2nd ed.). Needham Heights, MA: Allyn & Bacon.

Poverty's Palette. (2004). [Digital images]. *New York Times.* Available: http://www.nytimes .com/slideshow/2004/05/07/magazine/20040509PORT_SLIDESHOW_1.html

Scheurman, G., & Newmann, F. M. (1998). Authentic intellectual work in social studies: Putting performance before pedagogy. *Social Education, 62*(1), 23–25.

Stiggins, R. J. (1997). *Student-centered classroom assessment* (2nd ed.). Upper Saddle River, NJ: Prentice Hall.

Stiggins, R. J. (2008, April). *Assessment manifesto: A call for the development of balanced assessment systems.* Portland, OR: ETS Assessment Training Institute.

Texas Education Agency. (2010, May). Social studies TEKS. Available: http://www.tea.state .tx.us/index2.aspx?id=3643

Tomlinson, C. A. (2014). *The differentiated classroom: Responding to the needs of all learners.* Alexandria, VA: ASCD.

Webb, N. L., & others. (2005). *Web alignment tool (WAT).* Madison, WI: Wisconsin Center of Educational Research, University of Wisconsin–Madison. Available: http://wat.wceruw. org/index.aspx

Wiliam, D. (2011). What is assessment for learning? *Studies in Educational Evaluation, 37,* 3–14.

Index

Note: Page references followed by an italicized *f* indicate information contained in figures.

accessing information, technology for, 144–146

alignment. *See under* standards

Amador, Dalainy, 119

American Psychological Association (APA), 118–119

APA (American Psychological Association), 118–119

assessment. *See also* performance assessments, curriculum-embedded
  alignment with standards, 80, 90, 101–105, 158
  annotated quality example of types and purposes of, 189–195
  authenticity in, 89, 90–91, 92*f*
  checklist for, 83
  combining using types of, 68
  curriculum-embedded *vs.* self-contained, 84–87
  demonstrations, 67–68, 69–71, 72
  diagnostic, 73–74, 162, 189–190
  formative, 74–77, 76*f*, 81, 162, 190–194
  implications for curricular evaluation and creation, 78–81, 79*f*–80*f*
  information-recall assessments, 67, 69, 72
  performance assessments, 67–68, 69–71, 72, 162

assessment (*continued*)
  process assessments, 67, 68, 72, 193–194
  product assessments, 67, 69
  purposes of, 73–77, 76*f*, 81
  Stiggins on, 66–67
  summary, 81–82
  summative, 77, 81, 194–195
  tools and activities, 82–83
  types of, 67–68, 70*f*
  when to use types of, 68–72, 70*f*

Bennett, Steven, 120

Bloom's taxonomy, 4

Brookhart, Susan, 40

Calpin, Celestine, 120

Capuano, Christina, 120

CCLS (Common Core Learning Standards), 3, 47

CCSS (Common Core State Standards), 3, 35

checks for understanding. *See* formative assessment

coding learning experiences, 124, 130, 134

coding standards in curricula, 43–44, 59–60, 59*f*, 65, 90

collaboration, technology for, 146–147

Common Core Learning Standards (CCLS), 3, 47
Common Core State Standards (CCSS), 3, 35
content-area alignment with standards, 31–33
content areas, organizing centers in, 12–13
content learning experiences, 118–119, 162
content understanding. *See* formative assessment
Crawson, Jeanene, 47
curricula
    about developing, 173–175
    accessibility, 155–163
    assessed curriculum, 2, 5
    assessment recommendations, 78–81, 79*f*–80*f*
    checklist for, 172
    curriculum-embedded performance assessments, 99–109, 100*f*, 162, 195–198
    formal curriculum, 2, 3–4
    formats for housing, 155
    instructional resources recommendations, 151–153
    instruction recommendations, 128–133, 129*f*, 131*f*, 132*f*
    layers of, 2–5, 156–163
    learned curriculum, 2, 5
    as living document, 2
    operational curriculum, 2, 4
    organizing centers of, 15–20, 18*f*
    professional development and, 163–165
    quality unit example, 176–183
    resources listed in, 163
    standards recommendations, 33–35, 34*f*, 42–44
    student work connection, 165–171, 166*f*, 167*f*, 168*f*
    summary, 171
    taught curriculum, 2, 4–5
    tools and resources, 172
    unit example, 159*f*–161*f*
    units descriptions, in curriculum, 156–157
    units fully developed, in curriculum, 157–162

curriculum-embedded performance assessment. *See* performance assessments, curriculum-embedded

demonstrations, 67–68, 69–71, 72. *See also* performance assessments, curriculum-embedded
developmentally appropriate practice, 57–58
diagnostic assessment, 73–74, 91, 162, 189–190
dispositional learning experiences, 125–127
document-based questions, 73–74
Donovan, Gabrielle, 47, 48–53, 54

engagement, student, 112
essential questions, 13–14, 162
executive function skills, 4
expectations, and student work, 166–170, 168*f*

feedback, 171
Ferraro, Loretta, 47
Fire Island School District (NY), 47–56, 62–64, 63*f*, 128, 129*f*
formative assessment, 74–77, 76*f*, 81, 91, 162, 190–194
Fox, Kiera, 120

Gonzalez, Elvira, 16
Google Drive, 146–147
grade-level focus skills, 59–60, 59*f*
grading. *See* summative assessment
gradual release of responsibility, 58–59

Habits of Mind, 4
Healthy Me Unit quality example, 176–183

information-recall assessments, 67, 69, 72
Ingram, Joan, 120
instruction
    annotated quality example of, 199–201
    checklist for, 135
    coding in curriculum design, 124, 130, 134
    content learning experiences, 118–119, 162

instruction (*continued*)
    dispositional learning experiences,
        125–127
    engagement, 111–112
    implications for curricular evaluation
        and creation, 128–133, 129*f,* 131*f,*
        132*f*
    learning experiences, 115, 116–118,
        199–201
    learning targets, 113–115, 116, 117
    lesson descriptions, 113–118, 114*f*
    process learning experiences, 119–125,
        121*f*–123*f,* 162
    rubric for discourse, participation, and
        engagement (DPE), 121*f*–123*f*
    scripted lesson plans, 115, 116
    summary, 133–134
    tools and activities for, 134
instructional resources
    annotated quality example of, 201
    checklist for, 154
    guiding questions, 154
    implications for curricular evaluation
        and creation, 151–153
    listed in curriculum, 163
    materials, 149–151
    purpose of, and curriculum, 151–153,
        154, 162
    summary, 153–154
    technology, 143–149
    text, 136–142
    tools and activities, 154

Jackson-Cole, Thalia, 16

Kong, Joan, 16

Learner-Centered Initiatives, 48, 127
learners, focus on, 4
learning experiences. *See also* instruction
    about, 115, 116–118
    annotated quality example of, 199–201
    coding in curriculum design, 124, 130,
        134, 162
    content learning experiences, 118–119,
        162

learning experiences (*continued*)
    dispositional learning experiences,
        125–127
    elementary example of using, 129*f*
    lesson-analysis chart, 132*f*
    process learning experiences, 119–125,
        121*f*–123*f,* 162
    rubric for discourse, participation, and
        engagement (DPE), 121*f*–123*f*
    secondary example of using, 131*f*
LinkedIn, 148–149
Locatelli, Liz, 48

Magnotta, Laura, 16
Mannan, Filomena, 120
Marzano, Robert, 40
materials for instructional resources,
    149–151
McNulty, Karen, 47
metacognitive learning experiences. *See* dis-
    positional learning experiences
Miuta, Angela, 16

*National Standards for High School Psychol-
    ogy Curricula* (APA), 118–119
New York State K–12 Social Studies Frame-
    work, 3
Next Generation Science Standards, 3, 31–32,
    55–56, 60, 61*f,* 71
North Rockland School District (NY), 156

organizing centers of curricula
    about, 9–12
    annotated quality example of,
        184–186
    central ideas, 14–15
    checklist for, 23
    connecting school values and focuses
        with, 20, 21*f*–22*f*
    content areas, 12–13
    essential questions and, 13–14
    examples of, 9–12
    implications for curricular evaluation
        and creation, 15–20, 18*f*
    performance assessment alignment
        with, 101, 162

organizing centers of curricula (*continued*)
    in quality curricula example, 158
    summary, 20–23
    tools and activities, 23

Pennsylvania Learning Standard for Early
    Childhood, 69
performance assessments,
    curriculum-embedded
        about, 67–68, 69–71, 72
        annotated quality example of,
            195–198
        authentic audience and purpose in,
            89, 90–91, 92*f,* 105–106
        checklist for, 110
        congruence and strong alignment to
            standards, 88, 90, 101–105, 162
        curriculum-embedded *vs.* self-con-
            tained, 84–87
        evaluation tool for, 100–108, 100*f*
        features of quality, 88–98
        implications for content areas, 98–99
        implications for curricular evaluation
            and creation, 99–109, 100*f*
        incorporating diagnostic and forma-
            tive assessment, 106–108
        measuring most important learning,
            88, 89–90, 101, 162
        opportunity for teacher feedback and
            student revision, 89, 91–93, 94*f*
        specific criteria for student perfor-
            mance in, 89, 93–98, 96*f*–97*f,* 108,
            162
        summary, 109
        tools and activities for, 109
Perrotta, Annamaria Giordano, 120
Picinich, Shannon, 47
Popham, W. James, 40
presenting, technology for, 147–149
process assessments, 67, 68, 72, 193–194
process learning experiences, 119–125,
    121*f*–123*f*
product assessments, 67, 69
professional development, 118, 163–165
publishing, technology for, 147–149

Ranieri, Teresa, 16
Rawlins, Shawn, 120
resources, instructional. *See* instructional
    resources
rubric for discourse, participation, and
    engagement (DPE), 121*f*–123*f*
rubrics, in performance assessment, 89,
    93–98, 96*f*–97*f,* 108

Scalia, Amaris, 156
school values, and organizing centers of cur-
    ricula, 20, 21*f*–22*f*
self-reflection, student, 68
skill understanding. *See* formative
    assessment
standardized testing, 67
standards
    about, 46–47
    across all units, 54–57
    addressed, 35–37
    addressed *vs.* taught *vs.* taught and
        assessed, 35–40, 39*f*
    annotated quality example of align-
        ment, 186
    annotated quality example of place-
        ment and emphasis, 187–188
    assessment alignment and, 80, 90,
        101–105, 158
    checklist for, 45
    checklist for curricular analysis, 65
    coding, in curricula, 43–44, 59–60,
        59*f*
    content-area alignment with,
        31–33
    curricular alignment with, 3,
        24–25
    curricular revisions and, 62–64, 63*f*
    degrees of alignment, 25–31, 27*f,*
        29*f,* 158
    developmentally appropriate practice,
        57–58
    grade-level focus skills, 59–60, 59*f,*
        158
    gradual release of responsibility and,
        58–59

standards (*continued*)

    implications for curricular evaluation
      and creation, 33–35, 34*f*, 42–44

    placement and emphasis, in curricula,
      48–53, 49*f*, 50*f*, 51*f*

    prioritization of, 40

    sequencing annually, 57–62, 59*f*, 61*f*

    summary of alignment, 44–45

    summary of placement and emphasis
      on, 64

    task alignment to, 25–31, 27*f*, 29*f*,
      158

    taught and assessed, 40–42, 53–54

    text choice and purpose of, 137–142,
      154

    tools and activities, 45, 65

state and national assessments, 60–62

Stiggins, Rick, 40, 66–67

Storybird, 146

student revision, in assessments, 89, 91–93,
    94*f*

student work, 165–171, 166*f*, 167*f*, 168*f*

summative assessment, 77, 81, 194–195

SurveyMonkey, 147

task alignment to standards, 25–31, 27*f*, 29*f*

teacher feedback, in assessments, 89, 91–93,
    94*f*

technology, for instructional resources

    about, 143–144

    for accessing information, 144–146

    for collaboration and interaction,
      146–147

    for presenting and publishing, 147–149

textbooks alignment, 35

texts, and standards, 137–142

Thinking Maps, 150, 152

Torres, Ramonita, 120

Twitter, 148–149

units

    evaluating and planning of, 15–20, 18*f*

    example, in curriculum, 159*f*–161*f*

    fully developed, in curriculum,
      157–162

    Healthy Me Unit quality example,
      176–183

    quality unit example, 176–183

    short descriptions of, in curriculum,
      156–157

    standards across all, 54–57

Venn diagrams, 152

Whelan, Dawn, 156

Williams, Hande, 16

About the Author

Angela Di Michele Lalor is a senior consultant at Learner-Centered Initiatives (LCI), where her work includes facilitating schoolwide initiatives in the areas of curriculum, instruction, and assessment. Her primary focus has been helping districts design high-quality units of study that incorporate meaningful and engaging learning experiences for students. In addition, she has worked with teachers to design quality assessments; link curriculum, assessment, and grading and reporting practices; differentiate instruction to meet the needs of all learners; and examine student work to move student learning forward. Her strengths lie in her ability to help groups of teachers work collaboratively to rethink and reflect upon their practices.

Angela has presented nationally at the ASCD Annual Conference. She published an article in the November 7, 2013, issue of ASCD Express entitled "Thoughtful Selection of Informational Text," which provides examples of how to use informational text within engaging and meaningful units of study. Her article "Keeping the Destination in Mind," in the September 2012 issue of *Educational Leadership*, includes practical tips and examples on providing students with effective feedback that will move learning forward.

Angela began her career as a 7th grade social studies teacher. She is a certified Fellow at Communities for Learning: Leading Lasting Change.

Angela is also an avid runner, having recently completed her second New York City marathon.

Additional information about Angela and her work is available on the LCI website (http://www.lciltd.org) and LinkedIn (http://www.linkedin.com/pub/angela-di-michele-lalor/7b/967/231). She can be reached at angelal@lciltd.org.

Related ASCD Resources

At the time of publication, the following ASCD resources were available (ASCD stock numbers in parentheses). For up-to-date information about ASCD resources, go to www.ascd.org. This book relates to the **engaged, supported,** and **challenged** tenets of ASCD's Whole Child Initiative; to learn more about this initiative, go to www.ascd.org/wholechild. Search the complete archives of *Educational Leadership* at www.ascd.org/el.

Print Products

Curriculum 21: Essential Education for a Changing World by Heidi Hayes Jacobs (#109008)

The Curriculum Mapping Planner: Templates, Tools, and Resources for Effective Professional Development by Heidi Hayes Jacobs and Ann Johnson (#109010)

Ditch the Daily Lesson Plan: How Do I Plan for Meaningful Student Learning? (ASCD Arias) by Michael Fisher (#SF116036)

Solving 25 Problems in Unit Design: How Do I Refine My Units to Enhance Student Learning? (ASCD Arias) by Jay McTighe and Grant Wiggins (#SF115046)

Upgrade Your Curriculum: Practical Ways to Transform Units and Engage Students by Janet A. Hale and Michael Fisher (#112014)

DVDs

Differentiated Instruction and Curriculum Mapping: What's the Fit? DVD by Heidi Hayes Jacobs and Carol Ann Tomlinson (#611019)

Getting Results with Curriculum Mapping DVD with Facilitator's Guide (#606167)

ASCD PD Online® Courses

The Common Core Standards and the Understanding by Design Framework: English Language Arts (#PD12OC002M)

The Common Core Standards and the Understanding by Design Framework: Mathematics (#PD12OC003M)

For more information: send e-mail to member@ascd.org; call 1-800-933-2723 or 703-578-9600, press 2; send a fax to 703-575-5400; or write to Information Services, ASCD, 1703 N. Beauregard St., Alexandria, VA 22311-1714 USA.

THE WHOLE CHILD

The ASCD Whole Child approach is an effort to transition from a focus on narrowly defined academic achievement to one that promotes the long-term development and success of all children. Through this approach, ASCD supports educators, families, community members, and policymakers as they move from a vision about educating the whole child to sustainable, collaborative actions.

Ensuring High-Quality Curriculum: How to Design, Revise, or Adopt Curriculum Aligned to Student Success relates to the **engaged, supported,** and **challenged** tenets.

For more about the ASCD Whole Child approach, visit **www. ascd.org/wholechild.**

WHOLE CHILD
TENETS

1 **HEALTHY**
Each student enters school healthy and learns about and practices a healthy lifestyle.

2 **SAFE**
Each student learns in an environment that is physically and emotionally **safe** for students and adults.

3 **ENGAGED**
Each student is actively engaged in learning and is connected to the school and broader community.

4 **SUPPORTED**
Each student has access to personalized learning and is supported by qualified, caring adults.

5 **CHALLENGED**
Each student is challenged academically and prepared for success in college or further study and for employment and participation in a global environment.

Become an ASCD member today!
Go to www.ascd.org/joinascd
or call toll-free: 800-933-ASCD (2723)

LEARN. TEACH. LEAD.

DON'T MISS A SINGLE ISSUE OF ASCD'S AWARD-WINNING MAGAZINE,

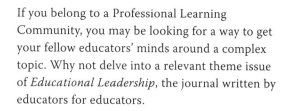

EL EDUCATIONAL LEADERSHIP

If you belong to a Professional Learning Community, you may be looking for a way to get your fellow educators' minds around a complex topic. Why not delve into a relevant theme issue of *Educational Leadership*, the journal written by educators for educators.

Subscribe now, or buy back issues of ASCD's flagship publication at **www.ascd.org/ELbackissues.**

Single issues cost $7 (for issues dated September 2006–May 2013) or $8.95 (for issues dated September 2013 and later). Buy 10 or more of the same issue, and you'll save 10 percent. Buy 50 or more of the same issue, and you'll save 15 percent. For discounts on purchases of 200 or more copies, contact **programteam@ascd.org**; 1-800-933-2723, ext. 5773.

To see more details about these and other popular issues of *Educational Leadership*, visit **www.ascd.org/ELarchive.**

LEARN. TEACH. LEAD.

1703 North Beauregard Street
Alexandria, VA 22311-1714 USA

www.ascd.org/el